EMPRESS EUGÉNIE:
Her Secret Revealed

By Joyce Cartlidge

EMPRESS EUGÉNIE: HER SECRET REVEALED
By Joyce Cartlidge
Editor: Kenneth Hite

Published by Magnum Opus Press
29a Abbeville Road
London SW4 9LA

ISBN: 1906402020
ISBN-13: 9781906402020

The photograph on p. 71 appears courtesy of Wigan Dept of Leisure. The quotations from the letters of Villiers, 4th Earl of Clarendon, on p. 192 appears by permission of the Earl of Clarendon. The Burgoyne letter on pp 196-198 appears courtesy of Peter Spencer. The author's photograph on p. 212 was taken by Muse Portrait Studio, Newark. Photographs of the Cartlidge family remain the property of their owners. All other photographs and illustrations are taken from sources in the public domain.

To Derek, Caroline, and Adrian
and
all of the other descendants of
Margaret Pemberton Cartlidge

Contents

The Empress Eugénie, painted by Claude Marie Dubufe in 1854

Introduction

'I should have liked to have gone to … the Empress's funeral. I suppose that very few people are alive today who saw her in her great days at the Tuileries. And I did. It was during my last Eton holidays, and I was asked to the last ball she gave before the waves closed over her splendour. She was radiant, without a jewel of any kind.

'Everyone else was emblazoned. The Emperor, half stupefied with morphia, inscrutable eyed, and mightily unimpressive. The Tuileries – now disappeared – gorgeous and crammed with the smartest and some beautiful women.

'The last time I saw the Empress was at the Savoy, lunching in the restaurant with some friends who had come over from France. She was an old woman, but all the beautiful lines of head and shoulders were still discernible. Her rise and fall are a romance quite unparalleled in history even in the short career of Ann Boleyn.'
    – Letter to 'L.B.' from Viscount Esher, 14th July 1920[1]

'Outside the Imperial entourage very little, probably nothing, is known of Her Majesty's private affairs. The Administer General, Mons Pietri, is a monument of discretion.'
    – Edward Legge, The Empress Eugénie and Her Son (1910)[2]

The Paris fashion house of Worth is still a familiar name, but how many remember Eugénie, the beautiful red-haired and Spanish-born Empress of the French, wife of Napoleon III, whose patronage made the Lincolnshire lad Charles Frederick Worth rich and famous? During the brief years of the glorious Second Empire and its extravagant court, lady guests of the Imperial couple were expected to change their dresses three times a day, and to wear no gown more than once during their stay.

After the fall of Napoleon, Eugénie, who became an intimate friend of Queen Victoria, spent the final fifty years of her long life in English exile, and travelling and sailing in her yacht, *The Thistle*. After 1891, she wintered in the house overlooking the sea that she had built on Cap Martin, a peninsula near Menton on the French Riviera.

She died on 11th July 1920 at the age of ninety-four whilst on a visit to her great-nephew the 17th Duque de Alba at his home the Liria Palace in Madrid. Her remains were brought back to England and interred in the Imperial Mausoleum at St Mary's Abbey which she had built very close to her home, Farnborough Hill, in Hampshire. She lies in the crypt with her husband the Emperor, who died in 1873, and with her son, the Prince Imperial, who was killed in the Zulu wars in 1879. At her funeral, Abbot Cabrol, referring to her long life, said 'a book would not hold it all', continuing, 'I hope that book will be written with all the scrupulous accuracy that history demands today.'[3]

Eugénie seems to have hoped for the opposite, and did her best to thwart any chance of 'scrupulous accuracy' in her chroniclers.

* * *

On 10th October 1895, at Abergeldie Castle on the Balmoral estate in Scotland, Sir James Reid, Physician to Queen Victoria, asked the Empress Eugénie if she had kept a diary. She replied, 'It is far better I did not keep a diary; there are things I could not have written down.'[4]

In January of 1910 she sent a letter to *The Times*,

stating that she had not written and never would write her memoirs. She reiterated this instruction in her will, requesting her executors to prosecute if any such memoirs appeared in her name.

When the author Lucien Daudet asked the Empress whether she would authorise him to write a book about her, she answered, 'Impossible! How could you write about me without giving new historical information, and as you know I always refuse permission for that. Surely you could not write without making me speak.' Nevertheless he wrote his book *L'inconnue* in 1911, and it is recorded that 'not a phrase displeased her'.[5]

However, she told Dame Ethyl Smyth that she would not comment on her biographies because 'nearly every statement was wrong'.[6] Smyth also asked Eugénie why she did not write her memoirs. The Empress replied cryptically, saying, 'People in a moment of infidelity failed you, who could show them up, but memoirs useless if this was not done'. In this strangely constructed reply Eugénie seems to be saying that she could not write her life story because she would have to expose some person or persons who had let her down, and unless she did so the memoirs would be worthless. Perhaps such a 'moment of infidelity' sparked her cynical words as quoted by Nancy N. Barker: 'It is rare in life not to experience deceptions, and it is always a cause of suffering to form attachments on this earth.'[7]

Ernest Alfred Vizetelly, a gossipy historical writer who called himself '*Le petit homme rouge*' ('the little red man') and who knew the Empress during her time in Paris, stated that 'she preferred to cast a veil over the past'[8].

Harold Kurtz, the biographer of the Empress, told of his enquiries on a visit to her home when he started his researches: 'Sir Alan Lascelles ... compiled an inventory of papers found at Farnborough [the Empress's house] in

1920. When Captain Lascelles first went to Farnborough in 1920, Bristol, the Empress's old major-domo warned him that he was unlikely to find much – the Empress had spent three days in 1919 burning papers!'[9]

Eugénie's habit of destroying papers was of long standing. Her turn of the century biographer Clara Tschudi reports that 'even after her hasty flight [from Paris in 1870] not a thing was discovered that could compromise her … the Empress of the French had always been careful of her reputation, for it is perfectly certain that she would have met with no mercy if it had been possible to sully her fair name.'[10]

Why such need for secrecy, considering her flamboyant lifestyle both as a young girl and when she became Empress of the French?

An interesting snippet, from the memoirs of Princess Caroline Murat, a contemporary of the Empress: 'When Gambetto Rockfort and members of the Government of National Defence searched the Tuileries [September 1870] they found a photograph of a handsome young man. Written on the back in Spanish – One must learn to love in secret.'[11]

* * *

My curiosity about the Empress Eugénie came about indirectly.

My husband Derek had never been able to tell me why his late father had Pemberton as a third Christian name. One day in my presence, he asked his father's elder brother Robert, a matter-of-fact man, who was a Garrison Engineer with the Royal Engineers stationed at Bicester near Oxford. Uncle Bob replied obliquely, saying that the Pembertons were supposed to be descended from the Empress Eugénie, and that he once made the mistake of mentioning this at school. Intrigued, I determined to ask more when I had researched this Empress, but Robert died shortly after and so my opportunity was lost. This family connection had apparently been a well-guarded secret, as my husband had never before heard it mentioned, although his father was alive until he was fifteen years old.

Uncle Bob's widow Jean had been very close to her father-in-law, keeping house for him for some years when he was a widower and her husband was serving in Singapore. Aunt Jean was reluctant to be drawn on the subject, saying only that the descent was 'through the mother, she was Spanish'. On a later occasion she warned me to 'be wary', adding that 'Bob was always evasive about the Pembertons'.

It is probable that Robert Cartlidge's black hair and Spanish appearance had led him to ask questions.

For the following two decades I was too busy with the current generation of Cartlidges to have very much time for family history, but I gained background knowledge by reading about the Empress and her period. Eugénie, unlike many other royal or aristocratic ladies of her time, did not write her memoirs. A reviewer of Kurtz's 1964 biography *The Empress Eugénie* asked, 'What was the Empress Eugénie's secret?'

Did I have the answer? When my children had grown I was able to concentrate on the mystery, believing that with the experience I now had in family history research I would quickly disprove this supposed descent from Eugénie. How wrong I proved to be! The more I discovered, the more probable the connection seemed to be. Not so much through available evidence but the through the unwitting testimony of missing records, notably at periods which were critical to my research.

Aunt Jean Cartlidge's remark that 'the mother' was

Spanish proved a red herring. My Pemberton-Cartlidge family history research concentrated on attempting to discover the origins of my husband's grandmother, Susan Helen Taylor, known to be a schoolmistress. Her birth was not registered and I came to a halt. After much research, I concluded that she was probably the illegitimate daughter of her 'father's' unmarried sister, also a Susan Helen Taylor. Her teaching records show that she added Susan to her name at the time of her supposed father's death, perhaps because at that time she met her natural mother.

My husband believed that the Cartlidges would be found in Staffordshire, and this is where I started my search. I discovered from the 1871 census that James Cartlidge, my husband's great-grandfather, was born in Astbury near Congleton in Cheshire and that he had married Margaret Pemberton at Christ Church, Pennington, Lancashire on 16 October 1859. Now I was getting somewhere. The 'mother' of whom Aunt Jean had spoken was in fact her father-in-law's mother, and not her husband's as I had assumed.

In the very early stages I visited the Stafford Register Office and was encouraged by the very helpful Registrar. That worthy's opinion was that on the face of it, the connection between the Cartlidges and the Empress seemed so highly unlikely that I should take it seriously.

I also investigated the possibility that the descent of the Cartlidges was not through the Empress but through her husband the Emperor. The future Napoleon III was a promiscuous man who had visited Birmingham and Lancashire in 1839. I found nothing at all to substantiate this theory.

Through the Family History Society I had the good fortune to make contact with family historian and Astbury resident Frank Cartlidge, who was most interested in my research and helped in any way he could. He told me that the family had lived in the village for at least four hundred years. Frank's great-grandfather and Derek's great-great-grandfather were brothers, sons of John Cartlidge (1782-1850) and his wife Mary (*née* Henshall).

At this stage came an interesting corroboration of the Cartlidge-Empress connection. My son, who was working in Staffordshire, met Barbara Perry *née* Cartlidge.

Mrs Perry told him that 'the Cartlidges were descended from the French "royal" family'. I had a telephone conversation with Mrs Perry, who told me that she had heard this through her father's uncle. Mrs Perry's Cartlidges are descended from William Cartlidge, son of John Cartlidge (born 1809), a farmer of Baddeley Green, Staffordshire. The two families may well have been distantly related since James's father Samuel was one of around twelve children born to John Cartlidge of Astbury, only 13 miles away from Baddeley Green.

* * *

The main part of my story examines the life of the Empress Eugénie, who was born exactly a century before me, almost to the very hour. The second part is based upon the life history of Margaret Pemberton.

Many biographies have been written about Eugénie, but other authors have not had my own advantage of family information. The validity of the connection between Eugénie and Margaret relies upon the very large number of coincidences involved, coincidences which go well beyond the bounds of probability.

The family information, personal names, occupations, places of residence, and significant dates of the Pembertons and the Cartlidges are the result of careful research. To make Margaret's story comprehensible and interesting

I have needed to make some assumptions about the day-to-day lives of the Pembertons and of Margaret's meetings with Eugénie. Unfortunately there are no letters or biographies of Margaret to study as there are for students interested in the Empress and her mother the Comtesse de Montijo. Of course, as with the journals and letters of Queen Victoria, Eugénie's letters were all carefully and systematically edited before historians ever saw them.

My research has been done purely out of curiosity. Family historians are often under suspicion of seeking out grandiose ancestors. We are, or should be, realists, prepared to accept the truths of history whatever they turn out to be. The past is already written and what has already taken place is unalterable.

I leave my readers to make their own judgement on the validity of my discoveries.

CHAPTER ONE

Eugénie: The Beginning

'The history of domestic relations cannot be written in the same way as the history of international relations, and any description of them must be tentative and incomplete.'
— Theodore Zeldin[12]

In the lovely Spanish city of Granada, the inhabitants were on edge. The air was heavy and still with an eerie silence. Experience told them that an earthquake was on its way. It was 5th May 1826, the fifth anniversary of the death of Napoleon Bonaparte. At No. 12 Calle de Gracia an aristocratic couple, Cypriano, Conde de Teba, the younger brother of the Conde de Montijo, and his wife Maria Manuela, prepared for the birth of their second child. Servants swiftly erected a makeshift tent in the garden to avoid any danger from falling masonry. In this romantic setting amongst the roses and cypress trees, the red-haired baby who would be named Maria Eugenia Ignatia Augustina arrived.

Cypriano, ten years older than his wife, had served in Napoleon's army as Colonel Portocarrero. After Napoleon's defeat in Spain, because of his French sympathies

Eugénie's parents
Cypriano, Conde de
Teba, and his wife
Maria Manuela,
Comtesse de Montijo

16

Cypriano spent several periods in prison. A striking looking redhead, he wore a black patch over a missing eye,
the result of an accident whilst proving a gun. In December 1817, in his thirties, Cypriano married Maria in the
southern Spanish city of Malaga, although as a nobleman
he had first to obtain the consent of the King. His bride
was the daughter of a Scotsman, William Kirkpatrick, son
of another William, himself the seventh child of a family
of nineteen children from the tiny village of Conheath
in Dumfries, Scotland. At the time of his daughter Maria's marriage Kirkpatrick was a fruit and wine merchant
in Malaga, where he had been the American Consul,
a position gained because of his French and American
sympathies. Maria's mother was socially superior to her
husband, as her father was a Belgian baron, Françoise de
Grivégnée, another Malaga wine merchant.

Maria and Cypriano had met in Malaga, where Maria
had acted as hostess for her father, and got to know each
other in Paris. Maria, dark-haired and attractive, was
typically Spanish in appearance. A linguist and musician,
she had been educated in Paris, a cultured woman by
the standards of her day. Cypriano was very careful with
money, but Maria loved the good things of life – perhaps
not a good combination.

The couple's elder daughter Maria Francisca de
Sales, known as Paca, was born in Santiago de Compos-
tela on 29th January 1825, where her father was being
held under house arrest.[13] Gossip suggested that she was
conceived during the time Cypriano was held in the grim
prison of Santiago, the implication being that he was not
her natural father.[14] Maria loved travelling, but had to
go abroad without her husband since Cypriano's freedom
was restricted, presumably for political reasons. It was acceptable and not unusual for aristocratic married women
to have lovers, and in Paris Maria had an affair with a

good-looking young Englishman, George Villiers, who is recorded variously as having sandy-coloured or very fair hair, blue eyes and a fair complexion.[15] Later to be Earl of Clarendon and British Foreign Secretary, Villiers was regarded as being Eugénie's possible father. He was living in Paris in the summer of 1825, the time of her conception, and admitted in a letter to Teresa, his sister, that he was 'being very wicked'.[16]

A letter dated 1st February 1852 to a 'Mrs G.' states, 'Regarding Charles's letters to George [Villiers refers to himself in the third person] strongly advise unless good reason to contrary destroy all during your lifetime – might not mind Teresa having them – not like them to fall in other hands advise after Teresa's death be burnt. George's letters at Teresa's death to be returned to us'.[17] This leaves no doubt that he was anxious about his earlier correspondence falling into the wrong hands. Portraits of the aquiline-featured Conde de Montijo, when compared with the rotund-featured Earl of Clarendon, favour Montijo as Eugénie's father. Eugénie made her appearance in French Imperial circles in 1852. In a letter sent to Teresa dated 9th September 1853, eight months after the Imperial marriage, Clarendon states 'I think that the anecdote that amused me most this evening was Madame Montijo telling [blotted] that after the Emperor's marriage was declared the Emperor shewed her a letter which had been written to him saying that his wife was George's daughter. The dame Montijo's answer was *"Sire, les dates ne correspondent pas."* He comments cryptically, 'Is that not that such?'[18]

Cypriano and his family lived in Granada until 1830, and during this period the couple had a third child, a son Paco, who lived only a few years. The children enjoyed the beautiful Palace of the Alhambra, which was close to their home. Here they listened with wonder to the tales told to them by their parents' friend Washington Irving, the American author of 'Rip Van Winkle' and other charming stories.

They also came to know Prosper Mérimée, a personable young Frenchman whose mother lived in Paris. He was a frequent guest of their parents. A Protestant, reputed to be an atheist, he was a man of varied talents. A student of law, he spoke fluent English and had many English friends. A respected archaeologist he became Director of Ancient Monuments for France. The story of *Carmen* based on a tale told to him by Maria Manuela was his work. He regarded Maria as his 'best loved friend in the world'[19] but his friends believed that 'he was not in love with her'.[20]

Mérimée took a great interest in Paca and Eugénie, as she was already known by then. (When very young she had adopted the French spelling of her name.) After the death of her husband, Maria took her troubles to him and he became the family's mentor. When Eugénie became Empress of the French she also turned frequently to him. At her urgent request, he edited her papers – as an old family friend, he was *au fait* with the family affairs and could be relied upon to remain discreet. His English was fluent and he had many English friends, one of whom was a lawyer, Sutton Sharpe. Sharpe, the son of a wealthy brewer, practised at Lincoln's Inn, London. He regularly received personal letters from Mérimée and would forward others to addresses elsewhere in England on his friend's behalf.[21]

The two men met regularly in Paris to enjoy the nightlife. Sharpe's fiancée Sophie Duvaucel was not included in their jaunts, unlike Mérimée's mistress Valentine Delessert, who often went along with them. Mme. Delessert had been married to Gabriel Delessert, Paris Prefect of Police, for five years when her relationship with

Mérimée began. Their two children Cecil, born in 1825, and Edouard, born in 1828, were playmates of Paca and Eugénie. Mérimée was 'uncle' to all four.

Cypriano's elder brother Don Eugenio held the titles Conde de Montijo and Miranda and Duque de Peneranda. He had been paralysed by a stroke and confined to a wheelchair. In this state, he was married in 1825 shortly before Maria, his sister-in-law, became pregnant for the second time. Eugenio's bride was a former prostitute who schemed to inherit the family fortune. She smuggled an infant boy from the local orphanage into her home, intending to pass him off as her own child and her husband's heir.

Maria, hearing of the 'pregnancy', became suspicious. Her family's prospects were in jeopardy, but at this time she and her husband were forbidden to travel for political reasons. A resourceful and intelligent woman, she arranged to be invited to a ball where the King of Spain was to be present and succeeded in charming him into giving her permission to leave home. Her unexpected arrival at her brother-in-law's house foiled the plot. She took the baby to her own home where he was cared for until he was grown up. Eventually he joined the army where his career was described as 'unremarkable'.

The invalid Conde de Montijo died in 1834. That same year a cholera epidemic took hold in Spain. Maria, the new Condesa, and her children hurriedly left for France but quarantine regulations stopped them at Barcelona. On the journey from Madrid Maria had befriended a famous young bullfighter, Francisco Sevilla, whom the authorities allowed into the city. Sevilla used his influence and enabled Maria, his new-found friend, and her three children to complete their journey, via Perpignan, to Paris.

Around this time the little boy Paco died, and Maria sent his sisters to school at the Convent of the Sacré Coeur in the Rue de Varrennes, the fashionable part of Paris. With the girls settled, Maria Manuela went back to Madrid, returning to Paris once again in July 1835, this time with her husband. Eugénie was particularly thrilled to be with her father again, as she was his favourite where her mother always preferred the calm and serious Paca. Eugénie's letters show that she had a great affection for Cypriano and when separated missed him very much. A lively child, her temperament matched her titian hair, always an embarrassment to her as the other children teased her. Her father understood, as he had suffered the same way himself. In order that she should not feel too much of an oddity, he employed a young gardener with hair of a stronger shade of red than her own. Whilst at their summer home Quinta de Miranda, in upper Carabanchel near Madrid, Cypriano regularly took his younger daughter out riding, presumably astride rather than sidesaddle. She became a fearless horsewoman with a passion for the outdoor life.

During their time in Paris the de Montijos lived as a family. Although by this time rich and elevated socially, the Conde did not indulge his daughters. Their spartan regime involved walking everywhere even though there were carriages available. When it was raining there were no umbrellas. The girls' simple dresses in winter and summer alike were of plain linen.

It was in Paris on 12th November 1836 that the future Empress was to have her first sight of the man she was to marry. In the company of her cousins the de Lesseps children, she was taken to see the young Prince Louis Napoleon as he was being transported for political interrogation following the Bonapartist putsch attempt known as the 'Strasbourg affair'.[22] This was an exciting event for Paca and Eugénie. Both their father and

Prosper Mérimée had told them tales of the great Emperor Napoleon, who had become their hero. This young Prince was his nephew.

After a short period at the Convent, Cypriano moved the sisters to a progressive school where physical training played an active part. The athletic and energetic Eugénie revelled in it. At home, the girls improved their English in conversation with an English governess, Miss Cole. On 25th March 1837 Eugénie took her first communion and on 5th May she celebrated her eleventh birthday. The 21st of the month was another landmark; Maria and her daughters left Paris for England where she enrolled the girls at a school for young ladies situated on the Royal York Crescent in Clifton, Bristol.[23] It was run by four sisters, the Misses Rogers, who arranged for the girls to attend the Trenchard Street Roman Catholic Chapel, the only Catholic church in Bristol.[24]

We have the reminiscences of Emily, Lady Clive Bayley, daughter of Sir Thomas Metcalf, who was sent along with her cousin, another Emily, to the Misses Rogers School in the spring of 1837.[25] She writes of a formal schoolroom, stiff schoolmistresses and, astonishingly, dry bread for lunch. Amongst her fellow pupils were her own Aunt Mary, Catherine (later Mrs Hamilton and mother of Lady Dufferin) and Ellen Caldwell, and also the two daughters of the Conde and Condesa de Montijo, who were staying nearby in a house in the 'Paragon'. 'Pakita' was, Emily says, very dark and handsome – typically Spanish. Eugénie she describes as a Scottish type with bright red hair and freckles. The two Emilys spent a lot of time with the Spanish girls who spent their afternoons at their home, and occasionally stayed for dinner – presumably served in the nursery, since they ate from a toy dinner service. The Spaniard's mother, the Condesa, whom she describes as jolly and good-natured, was an old friend of their aunt, who had recommended the school. Their father she described as evil-looking, because of the black patch he wore on his eye. Emily recalls that she was in school talking to Eugénie when she heard of the death of William IV on 20th June 1837.

The sisters did not enjoy England. Paca wrote home on 11th July 1837,[26] desperate for a visit from her parents. She told them that she found Clifton boring.[27] Eugénie was very unhappy because the other girls teased her calling her 'Carrots'. Two Indian princesses were equally miserable there; all three girls stowed away in a ship bound for India. Paca told her teacher, and the children were found before the ship sailed.

Maria rushed to Bristol when she heard what had happened, and in August removed her daughters. Fluency in English had been one reason for the choice of school; the alternative was a new English governess. Maria engaged Maria Juana Flower[28] probably from Pensford near Bristol and took her with her daughters to Paris. This time it was the usually placid Paca who became rebellious and gave Miss Flower a rough time. Presumably the Conde and Condesa were not at home since Prosper Mérimée went to sort things out.

At this time Cypriano was back in Spain and was obliged to obtain permission from the Queen Regent to return to Paris, where they had two houses, 24 Rue d'Angoulêm and 12 Place Vendôme. After only four months he was recalled, saying goodbye to Paca and Eugénie for what was to be the last time in January of 1838.[29] Maria left Paris shortly thereafter, although she could not have been lonely in Paris since her sister and her brother-in-law Matthieu de Lesseps lived there, as did her old friend Prosper Mérimée, who enlarged her circle with his own friends. Amongst them was Henri Beyle, the author better known as 'Stendhal' (1783-1842), who was

23

a weekly visitor to her home. Maria's first port of call was London, moving on to the various fashionable watering places.

In February 1839 Maria was back in Paris, where she received news of Cypriano's illness. She immediately rushed off to Madrid. Three weeks later on 17th March, Miss Flower received an urgent message from her employer instructing her to return the girls to Madrid as their father was deteriorating. They were too late. He died on the 19th, the sad news reaching them at an overnight stop at Oloron.

Stendhal, who was smitten with Paca and Eugénie, made a coded reference to their leaving Paris in a footnote to Chapter 3 of his novel *La Chartreuse de Parme*, which he was writing at the time: 'Para V P. y E. 15 X 38'. ('For you Paca and Eugénie 15 December 1838', 'X' apparently referring not to October but the Latin December.) A few days later in Chapter 26, another footnote read 'P y E in Olo' ('Paca and Eugénie in Oloron').[30]

Mérimée recorded that Eugénie was becoming a woman at the time she left Paris in 1839.

Paca and Eugénie would not return to Paris until they were grown.

CHAPTER TWO

Margaret: Beginnings

Betty, the daughter of a single girl named Ellen Parkinson,[31] was born at Tyldesley near Leigh, a cotton-manufacturing area lying midway between the port of Liverpool and the large industrial town of Manchester. She was baptised at Lady Huntingdon's Connexion, a Methodist chapel, in January 1813. When her daughter was seven years old Ellen Parkinson married Robert Redford, a cotton weaver who was twelve years her senior. Ellen and Robert produced four more daughters, Mary, Margaret, Charlotte and Alice. Their first-born child, a boy, had not survived.

By 1831 Betty Parkinson had found lodgings away from home at Bolton, some five miles away, where she worked in a cotton mill. In May 1834 Betsy, as she had now become known, married Robert Pemberton, the son of a cotton weaver named Joseph Pemberton and his wife Mary. The ceremony took place at St Peter's Church in Bolton. Although they had put up the banns, neither the bride nor the groom appeared to have any close relatives with them on their wedding day. The witnesses were Laurence Cooke and James Liptrot.

Robert and Betsy set up home at Atherton which was

just a mile or so from her mother, now Mrs Redford, at Bag Lane. Betsy's husband Robert had become an overlooker of power-driven looms at an Atherton mill. The power-loom overlooker was comparatively prosperous since his output was much greater than that of the hand-loom weavers.

Life was very hard for all the mill workers. Even little children worked up to fourteen hours a day in the factory. Conditions were unhealthy and there was little time or money available for much other than the basic necessities of life. Nevertheless, Lancashire people were warm-hearted and generous, helping each other in every way they could. Such social life as there was revolved around the church and the public house. When the weather was kind they would escape the streets and make their way up to the fresh air and peace and quiet of the nearby hills and moors for a few hours, looking down on the noisy towns with their coal mines and mill chimneys belching out smoke and dirt.

Betsy and Robert's first child, Nancy, was baptised in April 1836, but lived only a very short time. Another daughter, Amelia, was born in November of the following year.

Betsy and Robert's happiness at the birth of their second little girl did not last very long. They baptised her in March 1838, when she was four months old. Shortly afterwards a cholera epidemic spread through the town, and when little Amelia was only four months old Robert registered her death from the dreaded disease.

By Christmas of the same year Betsy and Robert knew that another child was on the way. It seemed a long while to wait until July — the third time would surely be lucky! As the warm summer days passed, it was usually humid in Lancashire and Betsy's pregnancy, by then in the latter stages, would have been tedious. Ellen, her mother, knew how important this coming baby was to her daughter, and insisted that Betsy came to stay with her and her stepfather until the new baby arrived. This third daughter was born at the Redfords' house early in July 1839, and named Nancy after the firstborn. Robert and Betsy did not wait so long this time before arranging a baptism. Nancy number two was just a few days old when the ceremony took place on Thursday 11th July 1839 at Atherton. Despite all their care she died at her parents' home at Tyldesley in November 1839. The next day Robert registered her death from 'debility'. He signed the register himself – this was a time when although it was not unusual to be able to read, very few ordinary people could write.

Towards the end of 1840, a year after Nancy's death, the local vicar on his rounds called on the Pembertons. He told them that he had been asked by Sir Henry Duckinfield, vicar of St Martin-in-the-Fields in London – known to the Leigh people because his family were local land and property owners[32] – to make enquiries about finding a suitable couple to adopt an infant. Sir Henry had a reputation for good deeds; he was 'associated with many acts of usefulness and benevolence'. He married twice and fathered 24 children,[33] and Robert Pemberton was 'an upright honest man and highly respected'.[34]

*The young Eugénie and her
older sister Paca*

CHAPTER THREE

Eugénie:
The Missing Year

'She (Eugénie) was in every sense of the word a spoiled child who had never been restrained in any of her fancies by a mother who was not overparticular or judicious.'
  – Anna Bicknell, Life in the Tuileries[35]

Eugénie's claim in 1877, when she was 51 years old, to have forgotten the year of her dangerous adventure was convenient considering that those who knew her well said, 'She had a prodigious memory, remembered everything',[36] and, 'Her memory was remarkable at a great age, never forgetting the smallest detail'.[37]

By August 1840 Eugénie was back in Madrid with her mother. Maria had the reputation of being frivolous and immoral. She loved the theatre and the opera, and lived life to the fullest. When at home in Madrid she would take home any young man who took her fancy. With her friends she played childish racing games around the house, astride their young 'captives' who cavorted about on all fours playing horses. The licence, amazing even for privileged aristocrats which Maria gave to her daughters is in keeping with her character. The deposed Empress

29

would later reveal a glimpse of her youthful freedom to Comte Joseph Primoli, her late husband's nephew and her friend, during a visit with him to Ronda in Spain in 1877.

The Comtesse des Garets, one of her 'Maids of Honour', recalls this 1877 visit to Ronda, and the local custom known as *pelar la pava*, translated literally 'to pluck the turkey hen'. The young girls stayed indoors in the daytime, leaving home to join their lovers between the hours of 10 P.M. and 2 A.M., after their parents were asleep. 'Here and there on the roads of Rhonda their silent silhouettes were to be seen'.[38] It was on this occasion, with young love so much part of the atmosphere, that Eugénie told Primoli of her own adventure.[39] It had taken place one hot July when, along with her sister and some other friends, she stayed out in the countryside for forty days and nights. During this adventure they encountered a band of Carlist rebels led by the notorious Pimentero.

Eugénie's recollections were published in *Revue des deux Mondes* in 1923. According to this article Eugénie, her sister Paca, her future brother-in-law the Duque de Alba, her cousin Pepe the Marquis de Alcañices (later to become the Duque de Sexto) and other friends were out hunting on Alba's estate.

They knew that there were bandits in the area (even then being sealed off by the police), but their excitement got the better of their judgement and they continued on their jaunt. Prepared for camping out, they spent their first night at the castle of Romanille, or Romaniglia, which was owned by the Duque. (The ruins of the Roman town of Italica are 9 kms west of Seville, where the Albas had a palace.) After a long ride and the necessary attention to their mounts the youngsters slept until two in the morning when they were woken by guards who told them that Pimentero was camped nearby with the intention of capturing the young aristocrats and holding them to ransom.

They rapidly packed up, saddled their horses in the moonlight and disappeared through a side gate into the countryside. They took refuge from the midday sun by a stream, and by evening they had reached a small village. However, the villagers turned them away, concerned that the nobles' presence would attract the Carlist bandits. They spent another night in the open, taking turns acting as lookout.

Eugénie told Primoli of one evening when she was at the rear of the party and fell asleep in the saddle, sliding to the ground without waking and continuing to sleep where she fell. After several hours she awoke and found herself alone apart from her horse, which was grazing nearby. Her friends did not hear her calling to them, but she found a track and caught up with them, giving vent to her anger on arrival. The response she received was hearty laughter; her friends asked whether she knew what she looked like. Her face was scarlet and she had a rash. Eugénie's explanation was that she had slept on moss, causing a reaction.

The party continued their travels despite being followed by the bandits and the risks of being taken prisoner. Eventually they reached Burgos where they found the town fortified and the gates shut. The young people were allowed entry and the gates closed were behind them. At this point the bandits gave up the chase and retreated.

The bandit chief later turned up at the gates of the Liria Palace in Madrid, the home of the Duque de Alba, and asked to see him. Alba agreed and the bandit asked for his respects to be given to the valiant horses which were unable, he said, to keep up with his mules. The Duque treated the man with courtesy, showed him round his stables, and 'never thought for a moment to denounce to the police the man from whom he and his friends had fled for forty days and nights'.

* * *

When Count Joseph Primoli asked his aunt the precise year of this adventure, Eugénie (renowned even in old age for her remarkable memory) replied 'How can I know? In Spain, these revolutions came about so frequently, that one counted them in months: it was during the July revolution….'

1840 was notable as politically stormy in Spain. This was the year that the Regent, Maria Christina, was forced into exile and General Espartero came to power. This ties in with Eugénie's statement to Primoli that the year of her outdoor adventure was also the year of an uprising. 1840 also agrees with Mérimée's letter written on 2nd August 1840 when he refers to 'brigands in the north and the invincible victorious duke'.[40] A letter from Maria, Condesa de Montijo to Stendhal, the only one of hers to have been published, is dated 27th June 1840. Writing at her summer home outside Madrid, she says she wishes to protect her girls from the ungodliness of the revolution and wishes she could make a long journey with them, but says she can't get away.[41]

The evidence makes it apparent that the year of the revolution and the youngsters' adventure was 1840. It would be a memorable year for more than a brush with revolutionaries. The events of that summer also explain Eugénie's reluctance, and that of her friends and relatives, to draw attention to the critical and embarrassing year between the summers of 1840 and 1841.

In 1931, Paca's grandson the 17th Duque de Alba (1878-1953), Eugénie's great-nephew and her confidante in her latter years, published a biography of the Empress by his friend the author Robert Sencourt (the *nom de plume* of Professor Robert Esmond Gordon George) written with Alba's co-operation. This book, Alba stated in a lecture he gave in Oxford in 1941[42], was the best biography of his great-aunt ever to have been written. But it seems remarkably, even conveniently, slipshod in the matter of dating Eugénie's early life. (The Duke of Alba later became a close friend and ardent supporter of Adolf Hitler, an interesting aspect of his personality.)[43] The biography says, 'She wanted to be back in Paris to see the arrival of the ashes of Napoleon from St Helena. But for a year or so she and her sister were sent to school in England.'[44]

The remains of Napoleon returned to Paris to be buried in Les Invalides in 1840.

Schoolmates met her mother and her father in Bristol in the spring of 1837. The Comte de Montijo died in 1839. Sending the sisters to England at the wrong time conveniently obscures 1840 to 1841. Page 43 of the Sencourt biography quotes a letter from Paca to Stendhal referring to a visit to Toledo and dates it as written 'prior to the girls going to Bristol'. The editor of Stendhal's correspondence dates it to December 1840, and dates another letter of Eugénie to Stendhal ('I had great pleasure in receiving your letter a little before leaving for Toledo') to the same year.[45] Alba said in this same lecture that the few errors in the book had been corrected in the French version. Nonetheless, in the French edition the content regarding this episode remains the same.[46] In another lecture about Eugénie that he gave at Barcelona University in 1947, Alba made no mention at all of her time at school in England.[47]

Not only Alba's biography, but the correspondence of her friends and relatives, leaves this critical period in the life of Eugénie almost blank. The Alba Archives in the

Liria Palace, Madrid, holds letters of Madame de Montijo, but the printed contents list none written before 1860. Gabriel Hanotaux of the Acadamie Francaise, editor of Eugénie's *Lettres Familières*, comments in that book that apart from one highly emotional letter dated May 1843, not a single letter remained in the archives for the period November 1838 to March 1849.

In Mérimée's letters to the Delessert family, the introduction comments that there is not one letter dated 1841 from Mérimée to the Delesserts.[48] The papers of Sutton Sharpe,[49] Mérimée's English lawyer friend, have a similar gap. Between 1836 and October 1842 there are no letters to the Mérimée family. The letters from Mérimée to Sharpe also have gaps in sequence between 1840 and 1841. Mérimée's letters to the Laborde family have gaps between 1840 and 1841: i.e., a letter to Madame Alex de Laborde dated September 1838, then one to Leon Laborde dated 'about 1840', another on the same vague date, and the next not until 2nd May 1842.

* * *

The conveniently forgotten date is far from the only thing about Eugénie's adventure that doesn't add up. Recall the episode when she vanished from the party, to appear later red-faced and disarrayed. Falling from her horse without knowing and continuing to sleep for half the night is ludicrous. Did her friends not get together for an evening meal? And would they not have missed her?

Marie des Garets, the Empress's young companion from 1868 when her mistress was 42 years old, refers to her mistress's impetuous and passionate nature: 'I never cease to point this out'.[50] How much more impetuous and passionate might she have been at age fifteen? Prosper Mérimée had commented sixteen months earlier when she had left Paris that she was becoming a woman.

One of the young people on the outdoor adventure in the summer of 1840 was José-Isidro Perez Osorio y Silva, Marquis de Alcañices, later to be the Duque de Sexto, known in Madrid society as Pepe de Alcañices. He was of ancient family, claiming descent from the medieval King Alfonso XI (through his lover Leonora de Guzman), but was just one year older than Eugénie. He lived in Madrid when the de Montijo sisters were in their early teens. He was believed to have been only interested in Paca, but would any normal young man in such circumstances be likely to have refused sexual advances made to him by an attractive and passionate admirer?

The Infanta Isabel was born in 1851 and was the half-sister of King Alfonso XII of Spain. Her daughter Princess Pilar of Bavaria quotes her family sources as saying that Pepe 'was the only man Eugénie ever loved … the lasting passion he inspired in the heart of Eugénie he could not return as he loved her elder sister, Francisca.'[51] Her account continues: 'After Napoleon proposed marriage to her she kept him waiting for an answer until she had written to Alcañices to say that if he would have her, with or without love – but with mutual respect – she would refuse Napoleon. Yet this is the woman whom so many writers have portrayed as merely an ambitious worldling ready to sacrifice anything if only she might wear a crown. She accepted Napoleon and the throne but only because the highest was not within her reach, and her bitterest enemies admit that thereafter, in spite of her consort's unfaithfulness, she never looked at another man.'

Other sources agree: 'Eugenia is in a passionate love with Pepe Alcañices,' quotes Maria's biographer Félix de Llanos y Torriglia.[52] Charles Petrie writes that 'the Duke of Sesto [Sexto] was the only man Eugénie ever loved,

*José-Isidro Perez Osorio y Silva, Marquis de Alcañices,
informally known as Pepe de Alcañices, and the man
said to have been the love of Eugénie's life*

[and] when Napoleon III proposed she kept him waiting until Sesto's answer to her letter.'[53]

Even Alba's book confirms it with an anecdote: 'You never would marry me', Eugénie said to Pepe when they met in old age and both were widowed. 'No, not even today', he retorted.[54]

* * *

Eugénie's story continues through Mérimée's letters to her mother Maria, the only documentary evidence discovered for the highly critical period.

Between 31st August 1840 and 22nd May 1841 Mérimée was writing more frequently than usual. The Empress found these letters, which contain many cryptic remarks out of context, in her mother's house after her death and brought them back to England.[55] Her great-nephew, the 17th Duque de Alba, published them twenty years after her own death.[56]

Why she had not burned these letters along with so much else is a mystery. Did she intend the truth to emerge in the future or, more likely, did she believe that the hidden messages would never be discovered?

Mérimée had been highly discreet in writing so cryptically. Even so, mail transported by messengers was insecure, even (or especially) for the highest nobility. Queen Victoria, when writing to her eldest daughter, cautioned her that she had to be careful what she wrote in case her letters were tampered with.[57]

Significantly, we do not have Maria de Montijo's replies. According to Primoli, Madame de Montijo's replies to her old friend's letters at this critical time were burned in Mérimée's Paris house fire. This fire broke out after Mérimée fled to Cannes in 1870 following Napoleon III's defeat at Sedan. The Empire was falling, and the Empress

Eugénie, the girl he had known since childhood, was in terrible danger. It seems more likely that Mérimée would have destroyed these letters himself before he left in order to prevent them falling into the wrong hands, or, if not, carried them away with him amongst his personal papers. At any rate, we do have parts of one side of the correspondence during the mysterious year 1840-1841.

On 31st August 1840, writing from Madrid, Mérimée replied to a letter from Madame de Montijo. She had evidently been asking him for some more 'graines'. He told her that these would not be available for 25 days Françoise Pate, a Frenchwoman married to an Englishman, who checked this section of translation, suggested that Madame de Montijo could have been requesting seeds for use as an abortive agent. Culpeper's *Herbal and English Physician* (a 17th-century herbal that went through over forty editions over the next 300 years, still in common use in the mid-19th century) advises 'grains of paradise' to help those whose courses [menstrual periods] are stopped',[58] an oblique reference to its abortifacient properties. Hemp was also used to ease the pains of childbirth.[59] *Graines de lin* or linseed is another possibility, as a second pressing of linseed oil was sometimes used as an abortive agent. Comte Fleury refers to the seeds in his *Memoirs of the Empress Eugénie*[60] as paulownia, which is used as a remedy for menstrual pain.[61]

In a letter from Madrid, dated only 'September 1840', Mérimée tells Maria that 'it was too late to deliver the letters for the English courier to carry tonight'[62]. Evidently Maria had urgent mail for England. Mérimée had become Maria's sole trustworthy link to England after the marriage of Lord Clarendon, her former lover and Eugénie's possible father. He had married Lady Katherine Barham, the widowed daughter of the Earl of Verulam, on 4th June 1839. On hearing this news Maria had sent him sarcastic letters.[63] It is not surprising, then, that she did not directly approach him in the summer of 1840.

Whatever this urgent news for England was, it was evidently distressing in the extreme. Mérimée says he is completely downcast, and refers to the 'moral discomfort of your friends – the worst thing they have ever heard'.[64] There are no recorded deaths in Maria's family at this time, and no great change in their fortunes. In the light of Maria's sudden interest in pharmacology, what could this 'worst thing' have been other than the pregnancy of Eugénie after her unsupervised 'adventure' in the wilds with her one true teenaged love? Pepe, the impulsive 16-year-old Marquis, did not want to marry Maria's daughter. Eugénie's marriage prospects, and perhaps Paca's, and indeed the entire social future of her family, were in jeopardy. Another letter from Mérimée at Burgos, dated 13th October 1840, says: 'Your dear children worry me very much, for themselves and for you to whom they are everything. Make them have your courage and good sense because I am very much afraid that they will have great need of both.'[65]

On 5th December 1840 Mérimée informed Maria Manuela that he was going to the 'Jardin des Plantes' for the seeds[66]. According to Raitt, his biographer, who seems to have the wrong idea, this so-called 'garden' was not the famous Paris botanical establishment, but really a book-strewn apartment where Merimée's friend Charles-Frederic Cuvier (1803-1893), a zoologist, entertained his friends on Saturday evenings.[67]

Around this time, Eugénie's family apparently visited Toledo, as we have seen earlier. Paca, the elder sister, wrote to Stendhal from Madrid in December 1840, telling him that she had been unable to write for a long time, as her family had been in Toledo.[68] The Alcañices had apartments within the castle of Toledo; perhaps they were sympathetic to her plight and gave Eugénie sanctuary and concealment. A letter written by Paca to Mérimée dated December 1840 bears a curious editor's footnote that 'this letter was sent through Captain FL Pleadwell.'[69] A later reference states that Pleadwell was 'M.D. Honolulu'.[70] A doctor? A letter from Mérimée written on 9th January 1841 to the botanist Adrien de Jussieu (1797-1853) asks for a repetition of glycinia seeds 'for a marvel in Madrid'[71]. What 'marvel' were they intended to perform? (Could this have been the 'atheist' Mérimée referring in jest to the upcoming 'virgin birth'?) It was surely too late for an abortion; perhaps they were needed as a rather more fragrant lubrication to ease the forthcoming delivery than the traditional hog's lard that the local peasants used for this purpose.

Writing from Paris on 12th February 1841, Mérimée tells Maria Manuela that he has not forgotten the 'graines'[72]. He still seems to be communicating in code when he states that he will come and visit when Paca gets married and wishes she (Maria) would look for a son-in-law in England but 'if England bores you, you will find English in Italy and in France'. He refers to 'her' as proverbially *'pobre porfiado'* ('self-willed and obstinate'). Was this a reference to Eugénie? He quotes another proverb, saying 'don't put too many eggs in one basket', suggesting that she should have more than one option in mind. He complains that Maria gives him no news of her *tertulianos* ('family circle') and ends with Mérimée sending his love to the senoritas, hoping that they have parties and 'get togethers'. He wishes for the *'senorita gachona'* (the 'sweet and spoiled one') a good-looking Englishman, a descendant of the Conqueror with beautiful lands in the county of Yorkshire. Llanos y Torriglia, the Spanish biographer of both Eugénie and her mother, asked whether the *'senorita gachona'* was the future Empress Eugénie.[73]

40

Mérimée may well have been referring to Eugénie's child, predicting a daughter with some connection to England.

The strangest reference of all in Mérimée's 12th February letter comes when he says that he is waiting with impatience for news of the suicide of the '*cornichon*' (the 'little ninny'). What could that mean? How could he have known in advance that a suicide was expected? Even assuming that he did, why would he be waiting with impatience for such news? Was Mérimée making a disguised reference to the pregnant Eugénie in saying that the hoped-for news — that the little ninny was dead and gone — meant that she had regretted the past and come to her mature senses?

Or was it a reference to a cover story even then under development? Although the Alcañices could keep Eugénie out of sight in their Toledo apartments, the family needed to explain her absence somehow. Sure enough, rumours were 'put about' of the young Eugénie attempting suicide by dissolving phosphorus matches in milk and drinking the mixture at some undated time. Versions of the story vary, and Eugénie's biographers have been unable to agree who or what was responsible for her well-documented but suspiciously vague 'suicide attempt'. After her death, her great-nephew the Duque of Alba stated that he believed the story of the suicide attempt, and that it was caused by her distress at his grandfather's forthcoming marriage to her sister.[74] This marriage took place in 1843, which makes Alba's theory yet another strand of misdirection around the period of 1840-1841. Further, unlike her infatuation with Pepe de Alcañices, there is no real evidence of an attachment on Eugénie's part to her sister's future husband.

Indeed, other sources do say that the cause of Eugénie's despair was her passion for Pepe Alcañices, who was not interested in her but used her to be near

Paca. The composer Dame Ethyl Smyth knew the Empress in her Farnborough days and accompanied her on a voyage on her yacht in early 1890. Comte Primoli, Napoleon III's nephew, was a fellow guest. It was on this holiday that Eugénie told them enough about her youthful adventures for Primoli to write his article 'L'enfance d'un souveraine'[75] and for Smyth to write about the suicide attempt in her book *Streaks of Life*. In Smyth's account Pepe was brought to Eugénie's bedside after her attempted suicide. Rather than commiserating with her or offering her hope, he asked her what she had done with his letters, which he had apparently written passionately. During this interview, Pepe disclosed his true interest in Paca, 'and so, disillusioned by his callousness, [Eugénie] swallowed the antidote'.[76] Even if she was aware of it, Smyth gave no indication as to how very young Pepe and Eugénie were at that time. In short, the 'suicide attempt' appears more like a cover story, with the seemingly convincing details added perhaps as much as fifty years later.

A few days later, on 20th February 1841, Mérimée wrote asking whether 'Madame X' had arrived[77]. By this point, six or seven months into Eugénie's pregnancy, it would be the right time to engage a wet nurse. The editor of Mérimée's correspondence states that 'Madame X' was Maria's friend, Madame Xifre y Casas whose husband was a very wealthy merchant with 'a fortune of "cinq cents millions de pesetas"'.[78] In the light of subsequent references to Madame X, this seems unlikely. For instance, two years later, on 24th February 1843, he wrote to Maria telling of giving Madame X 239 francs 50 (around £6 in 1840) for 'memoirs'. Was this hush money? Evidently these memoirs, whether oral or written or merely potential, were important. If Madame X were a hired nurse, then to her it would be a substantial sum: by the turn of the century the average wage in Paris was 170 francs per month. He would not be buying off the wealthy Madame Xifre with what, in any case to her, would be a paltry amount. In the letter, Mérimée reminds Maria that she should have been given a receipt, again hardly the sort of request to be made to a wealthy friend for a comparatively small sum. Three months later a letter dated 27th May 1843 refers once again to Madame X 'to whom you have given money'.

Merimée finishes the 20th February 1841 letter by asking again whether the 'cornichon' was dead. Was he really asking if the 'ninny' was gone or reformed?

On 12th March 1841 Mérimée asks Maria for an address to send 'dahlias'.[79] A later letter suggests that they were for Maria's own garden. Why should her old friend need an address when he had so frequently visited her home and knew it well?

By 2nd April he writes an obviously coded message[80] saying that he is getting very worried about the dahlias because they seem to have waited rather too long. He sends instructions to Lucas, the family's major-domo, concerning the transport of the 'dahlias' to Madrid in a game basket, on the way to the de Montijo summer home at Carabanchel just outside the city. A lidded basket would be a secret and convenient way to move an infant, perhaps one sedated with suitable seeds or 'graines'.

Merimée goes on to say that he approves of the de Montijos spending Easter, which fell on 11th April that year, in Toledo, forty miles south of Madrid[81]. There was a convenient tradition that pregnant women who ascended and descended the (then) thirteen steps of Toledo cathedral were ensured an early and easy delivery. Did Eugénie remain there whilst her mother and sister returned to Madrid in November?

On 8th May 1841 Mérimée wrote from Paris a long letter to Maria, saying, 'I hope that the dahlias [the in-

Prosper Mérimée

fant?] have not suffered travel fatigue which could have affected their delicate constitution'.[82] He goes on to say that he has received a letter with many impertinences from Madame X. Again, surely he means the wet nurse and not his and Maria's mutual friend, Madame Xifre! The letter continues, saying that he had met, at the house of 'Lady Helen' [Robinson?], a magnificent young English aristocrat whom, he said, had everything. The young man intended to go to Spain and Mérimée had hopes that he would 'deviate' Paca's love life. 'Don't tell Paca', he says, 'that we look for husbands over the sea or she will dislike me'.[83]

Although Mérimée's well-meant match-making came to nothing in this case, it does demonstrate his continuing connection (and possible travels to) England during this time. He then says, 'I very much approve of the journey to Bilbao'[84], a busy seaport in northern Spain. Mérimée suggests to Maria Manuela that if she is going as far as Bayonne, a French frontier town beyond Bilbao, she should go on to Paris[85]. The plan appears to have been that Lucas, the major-domo, and Madame X, the wet nurse, would take the newborn infant to Madrid from Toledo en route for Bilbao in northern Spain. Maria, showing the same determination to protect her family as she had when her brother-in-law's wife had attempted to pass off an orphan as the legitimate heir, travelled as far as Bilbao with Madame X. Here they parted company, Madame X making the sea-crossing to Liverpool while Maria travelled on to Bayonne.

Mérimée ends his letter by sending love to the girls and to 'the innocent victim who breathes under your protective roof', confirming that the infant, referred to with due compassion, had, allowing a few days for Mérimée to receive the news, been born about 4th May 1841. (Thus the date of Eugénie's 'adventure' would likely have been early August or late July 1840.) It was customary for Catholic infants to be baptised immediately. Did the grandmother place a gold chain around the child's neck, as she did at the baptism of Eugénie's legitimate child, the Prince Imperial?

At this time Eugénie's future was an unknown quantity. Maria could not have guessed that her daughter would become an Empress. She may have hoped that it would one day be possible to reclaim her grandchild, but the conventions of the day considered it bad taste and reprehensible for illegitimate children to acknowledge their parents.[86]

On 15th May 1841 Mérimée wrote to Maria saying that he had a word for Madame X, whom he supposed was with her again[87]. By this time, she should have handed over the baby to the foster parents in England and returned to Spain. On 22nd May he wrote, 'I hope you executed your project at Bayonne,' but gave no clues as to what this 'project' might have been, and says that he presumes his friend Maria is accompanied once again by Madame X who appears to have been delayed. On 29th May he makes a reference to the route to Bayonne.

A very strange remark is contained in Mérimée's letter written seven days later: 'I am happy that your dahlias are in good health – you know if you plant them apart one from the other, as with potatoes one can keep them from one year to another'[88]. He had previously referred to 'dahlias and their delicate constitution'. He seems to be reassuring Maria that since both mother and child were in good health, each could thrive, even though they were apart.

CHAPTER FOUR

Margaret: Without a Mother

'It was the custom of the time in Spain for the illegitimate offspring of unmarried girls from the wealthy class to be farmed out to poor mothers, preferably those who had lost their own child and whose maternal instinct was strong. They received payment consisting of about eight shillings a month. If there was any possibility that the child would one day be reclaimed, it would be given an ornament or other memento to enable it to be identified.'
    – Richard Ford, Gatherings From Spain[89]

In March 1855, writing some years after the mysterious events of 1840-1841, Prosper Mérimée made the point that 'everyone is good in Spain – when the poor girls find themselves "comme il suit", they give the newly born infant to a faithful chambermaid who disposes of it in the night.'[90] Customs were much the same in England. The Manchester paper *Lloyds Weekly News* regularly carried advertisements from people wishing to foster young children. Eighteen pence to three shillings weekly was the going rate. Conditions were in many cases appalling and a large number of the babies died.

For an aristocrat a more likely method of obtaining a suitable foster mother in a distant place would have been with the co-operation of a sympathetic clergyman. Through his friend the lawyer − later to be Q.C. − Sutton Sharpe, Prosper Mérimée knew of just such a cleric. Sharpe also knew Maria de Montijos; all three had dined with Stendhal in Versailles in the autumn of both 1837 and 1838.[91]

Sharpe practised at Lincoln's Inn in London, and lived at Nottingham Place. Midway between Lincoln's Inn and Nottingham Place lies St Martin-in-the-Fields, where the vicar from 1834 to 1848 was Sir Henry Duckenfield. Though his family originated from Cheshire the Duckenfields also held property in the adjoining Leigh district of Lancashire. They owned Atherton Hall, situated midway between Atherton and Leigh, and also were landowners at nearby Bedford.

Atherton, Tyldesley, Pennington and Leigh are small towns grouped together in the registration district of Leigh, thirteen miles from Manchester. Leigh was well placed to receive traffic via Manchester from Liverpool. As early as 1841 there were three alternative modes of transport: the regular timetabled packet-boat service based at The Old Packet and Boat House, a horse-drawn coach service from the White Horse Inn, and also one of the first railway passenger services in the world.

From the sixteenth century onwards there had been regular shipping trade from Bilbao to Liverpool. In the 1840s ships delivered streams of Spanish iron ore to England, returning loaded with cotton goods. After docking at Liverpool a journey could be made by canal into Manchester and beyond. Manchester had many Spanish business houses, and the mail from Spain arrived regularly each Monday, providing an easy and convenient way of paying maintenance.

Thus Leigh was far enough away from Spain to avoid scandal, but thanks to the ever-tightening industrial and commercial world of Victorian Europe, it was close enough for news — and if need be funds — to travel at need.

* * *

With his Lancashire connections, Sir Henry would have known whom to ask about providing foster care to a newborn. In Atherton, the local vicar knew Betsy Pemberton and of her grief at losing her three daughters. She was herself the child of an unmarried mother and needed no persuading to give a home to the baby. Milk for the infant would be no problem as it was customary to acquire a nanny goat to provide it when the mother could not.

The details were arranged; Betsy and Robert Pemberton likely agreed to collect the baby at the Old Packet and Boat House Inn in Leigh, the terminus for the canal boats. They would register the baby immediately as their own child to remove from her the stigma of illegitimacy, and then move away. Central Manchester was only thirteen miles distant and there were plenty of jobs available for a skilled overlooker in the cotton mills. In another district no one would ever know that Betsy had not been pregnant.

On 18th May 1841 Betsy Pemberton registered Margaret, giving her birthplace as Atherton and the date of birth as 4th May. Betsy could not write and the certificate is verified with her cross.

This same month, Robert Pemberton's brother James and his wife Dinah (*née* Aldred), who were just 19 and 21 years old respectively, and who lived on Bag Lane near the Redfords, produced a baby girl who was also given the name of Margaret. This other Margaret Pemberton was baptised at Atherton on 8th August 1841, but no baptism has come to light for her 'cousin' of the same name. She was presumably baptised at birth in Spain, as was customary.

By census day on 7th June 1841 Robert, Betsy and Margaret had disappeared from the district They turn up at Cookhedge, Warrington, eleven miles away, with the infant Margaret correctly named but recorded as male. This move went against the local custom whereby the grandmother would care for the child while the mother returned to work. Both Margaret Pembertons have been located in the 1851 census: the daughter of Robert at 18 Trumpet Street, Deansgate, Manchester, and the daughter of James at Bag Lane, Atherton.

Betsy's joy in her strong little baby was to be short-lived, since by the end of 1842 she was seriously ill. Caring for Margaret and her husband became too much for her. She returned to Atherton and the care of her mother, Ellen Redford.

As we have seen, Robert Pemberton could read and write. Evidently Madame de Montijo had kept in touch with him and had requested that he let her know if there was ever any problem which would affect the well-being of her little granddaughter. She was not as heartless as her daughter believed. On receiving the news of Betsy's illness, Maria Manuela once more contacted her old friend and confidant, Prosper Mérimée.

It is at this time (24th February 1843) that Mérimée discusses the need to pay off 'Madame X' for her 'memoirs', implying that his renewed need for a messenger had aroused that worthy's greed. On 15th April 1843 Mérimée wrote in riddles once again to Maria from Paris, saying that Calderon was going to England and 'would do the business of financier well'.[92] This refers to Serafin Estabañez Calderon (1799-1867), the Spanish writer best known as 'El Solitario', and a friend of Maria Manuela. (Mérimée's previous go-between, Sutton Sharpe, had died on 22nd February following a stroke in December 1842.) On 9th May Mérimée reports to Maria that Calderon has returned, 'enchanted with England and the English'.

On 13th May 1843, Mérimée wrote from Paris in his by now usual cryptic fashion of Maria Manuela's 'foreign affairs' and of an 'agitated doctor who was not a beast and would know the outcome'. He refers again to Madame X, saying that it is a long time since he has seen her, and that he will write and ask her how to take the money. In a further letter to Maria dated 27th May 1843 Mérimée makes another vague, possibly coded, reference to Madame X, a householder, and money.

Calderon, whilst in England, had evidently visited the Pembertons and arranged to send financial help after learning from her doctor that Betsy had not very long to live. She was suffering from galloping consumption, a disease that developed rapidly. Its victims survived only a few short months from the onset.[93] Extra money would be very welcome at such a time and it would seem that money coming from Spain was to be handed over by Madame X.

In England on Sunday 25th June 1843, Betsy Pemberton died at her mother's home. She was just thirty years old. Her stepfather Robert Redford registered her death at Leigh Register Office on the 28th. Betsy was buried on Thursday 29th June after a service at the parish church of St George, in Tyldesley.

Betsy's mother Ellen cared for the baby Margaret until Robert Pemberton arranged for seventeen-year-old Abigail Barbara Landon to keep house for him. Abigail, the daughter of Thomas and Sara Landon, was born in

51

Manchester on 8th Jan 1827.[94] She was just nine months younger than Eugénie, whose child she was destined to bring up.

CHAPTER FIVE

Eugénie:
The Marriage
Market

'*[Eugénie is] an infuriating girl, who with childish playfulness, shrieks, makes a noise, and gets up to all the naughtiness of a six-year-old child. At the same time she is quite the most fashionable young lady of this town and court, and she is so short-tempered and bossy, so fond of physical exercise and the flattery of good-looking gentlemen, and, in short so adorably badly brought up that one can be virtually certain that her future husband will be a martyr to this heavenly, aristocratic, and above all, wealthy creature.*'
– *Juan Valera*[95]

In August 1842 Francisca (Paca) de Montijo's engagement to the 21-year-old Jacobo Luis Francesco Pablo Rafael FitzJames Stuart y de Ventimiglia, 8th Duke of Berwick and 15th Duque de Alba de Tormes, was formally announced by her mother.

Towards the end of 1842 Prosper Mérimée wrote to Mlle Daquin informing her that Madame de Montijo was coming to Paris to get her daughter's trousseau. The families planned the marriage for the spring of 1843.[96] Mérimée said he did not know the future son-in-law but commented in a letter to Mlle Daquin at the end of 1842 that he was once instrumental in having another suitor discarded: 'a poor wretch although a grandee several times over'.[97] Was he referring to Pepe, Marquis de Alcañices, who had seduced Eugénie although in love with her sister?

That spring Pepe, who was not the best of terms with his father,[98] still moved in the same social circle as the de Montijo girls. Mérimée, in Paris, read a report in *El Heraldo* of a Madrid party. Pepé, it said, had been seen dancing quadrilles with Paca and Eugénie. Mérimée commented, 'It seems that the Marquise had made the night a little dark in spite of all the spangling stars'.[99] He seems to be saying that Pepe's mother's presence must, for the two girls, have somewhat spoiled the evening. But in the event Paca's wedding was postponed until the autumn. Maria's excuse was that she had been unable to make all the arrangements in time, but the dates coincide with Betsy Pemberton's health crisis, and with a sudden and simultaneous bout of despair on Eugénie's part.

Just seventeen years old, Eugénie had been told that Betsy, her baby's foster mother, had not long to live. Worse, Betsy's sickness was known to be contagious. What if the baby caught the disease from her foster mother? The concern in the de Montijo household for the tiny girl's future welfare revived every trauma Eugénie had suffered following her 'adventure' in the summer of 1840. She had been rejected by her lover and forced into confinement. Never Maria's favourite, she had no doubt been lectured and hectored during the tense winter months. The chances that she suffered physical damage whilst giving birth at the age of fifteen were very great. As if all of this had not been enough for the girl to cope with, it was followed by the swift removal of her baby daughter, probably in the dead of night when she was asleep, a custom recorded by Mérimée.

On 13th May Mérimée wrote to Maria of an 'agitated doctor who was not a beast and would know the outcome'. (No doubt other letters, since destroyed, conveyed the terrible news more clearly.) Mérimée's letter of 13th May would have arrived in Madrid by the 17th. In her current emotional turmoil and her anxiety for the future of her two-year-old daughter, Eugénie had to confide in someone. The Duque de Alba was the obvious choice: he was about to marry her elder sister, he had been on the safari in the summer of 1840, and he knew everything.

On 17th May 1843 Eugénie wrote an emotional letter to Alba, the first letter since one dated 1838 to be published in her *Lettres Familières*.[100] (The next letter in that collection is one dated 1849.) Perhaps indicating her mental turmoil, she started this letter by making a mistake over the date, writing it as 'Tuesday May 16th', when in fact in 1843 Tuesday was the 17th.

The girl wrote of her misery and her passions and of how she had been beaten, presumably by her mother. She was regarded, she said, with indifference by everyone, even the man she loved most and for whom she would even have consented to her own dishonour. (Or was she saying she *had* so consented?) 'You know this man,' she tells Alba, not needing to commit the traducer's name to paper since Alba would know perfectly well that she meant Pepe. Previous biographers, either deliberately or accidentally muddying the waters, have stated (against all other evidence) that 'the man she loved most' was Alba himself. She continues by commenting that he does not know what it means to love someone and to be despised in return. She wishes him and her sister all happiness in their marriage and warns him not to lose the love of one

55

Paca de Montijo, the Duquesa de Alba

child by showing more affection to the other, an obvious criticism of her own mother. She ends on a dramatic note stating that she may end her days in some cloister.

A few days after Eugénie wrote this letter the Condesa de Montijo postponed Paca's wedding until autumn and took her girls to Paris for three months. Eugénie needed distracting, and because the wedding had been postponed Maria decided that the engaged couple should not be too much in each other's company. Perhaps learning from the events of 1840, Maria did not want Paca to become pregnant before her marriage. In Paris, where they stayed for three and a half months, they could concentrate on shopping for the trousseau. There also they met their good friend Mérimée again for the first time in three years. The change of scene worked wonders: Mérimée wrote to a friend on 24th June 1843 that all three de Montijos were in sparkling health.[101]

On their arrival home in Madrid, Maria made sure that an abortive agent was to hand in case Paca should need it. On 18th September 1843 Mérimée wrote to Jussieu, his botanist friend. He refers to the 'graines' sent previously by Jussieu to Madame de Montijo and tells him that she would welcome some more.

Paca and the Duque de Alba were married on 14th February 1844. Apparently Maria's new determination to rein in her daughters had not proved fully successful, as Paca was likely two months pregnant by then. In October of that same year Mérimée replied to a letter from Maria telling her that his mother, 'who knew about these things', said that a seven-month accouchment was not dangerous and that he hoped that this would be the case for 'poor Paca'. Madame Mérimée appears to have been reassuring the de Montijos that a (supposedly) two-month premature infant could survive. It is rather more likely that Mérimée and Maria had knowledge of a premature consummation than it is that they correctly anticipated a premature birth. On 26th October 1844, eight months after the marriage, Mérimée wrote again to Maria de Montijo saying that he had received her letter of the 19th and was very worried that the birth had not occurred. This letter was written a month before the child could have been expected to arrive if it had been conceived after the marriage.

Despite her mother's precautions the first son of the Albas was born, according to a footnote in Eugénie's published letters, 'in 1844, seven months after the marriage'.[102] Mérimée's letter to Maria written on 16th November 1844 refers to 'your little boy Carlos', but the child did not survive.[103] The eventual heir to the Duque de Alba, also named Carlos, was born on 4th December 1849. The couple also had two daughters: Maria Luisa, born in October 1853, followed just a year later by Rosario, also born in October.

Since Paca was now, as the Duquesa de Alba, one of Spain's highest-ranking nobility, her mother concentrated on the marriage prospects of her younger daughter. In 1846 mother and daughter did the social rounds, visiting Brussels and the popular spas of the day, before travelling on to London.

Eugénie was never short of suitors, but to her mother's dismay showed no interest in any of them. She gained a reputation for being frigid, although her more perceptive friends believed that an unhappy love affair in her youth had damaged her emotionally. No doubt they were right, but they could not know that she had also probably been injured undergoing childbirth at the early age of fifteen. Physically immature girls who become mothers at 14-15 years of age often receive internal damage to the bladder and bowels, in addition to any external or genital damage.

Eugénie had already rejected the son of William C. Reeves, the American Minister in Paris, the Duke of Orsuna, and Jose Xifre, the son of her wealthy friend. Another admirer was Ferdinand Huddleston, an eligible young Englishman who lived in a lovely 16th-century manor house, Sawston Hall near Cambridge. He was fascinated by the flamboyant Spanish girl and tried his luck. Mother and daughter accepted his invitation to stay at his home. He proposed, but both he and Maria were disappointed when Eugénie refused him. Maria's former lover George Villiers, by this time Lord Clarendon, was another host, together with his new wife, the daughter of the first Earl of Verulam.

At his home, the Grove at Watford, Eugénie joined the foxhunt. The conventional English black riding habit and silk top hat looked well on her auburn hair. With her fair skin and slim figure she looked the part of an English aristocrat, yet the formal clothing concealed a fearless Spanish horsewoman. As she led the field she enjoyed the sensation she created, perhaps wondering what the reaction might have been had she had been wearing her usual equestrian attire. On her way to the bullfights in Madrid she would be seen riding a spirited mount without a saddle, whilst flourishing a whip and smoking, looking superb in traditional Andalusian costume, her hair plaited and decorated with flowers and jewels. A dagger fixed in her belt and red satin boots on her feet completed the picture.[104]

After their journeying abroad, mother and daughter returned to Madrid, and in 1847 Maria was invited by the 17-year-old Queen Isabella II to become her Camera Major, or chief lady-in-waiting. *The Times* recorded her appointment on 12th and 14th April 1847. Isabella had ruled Spain since she came of age in 1843. Since 1840 political-minded generals known as Moderates or

Progressives had run the country. In 1843 the Moderate General Narváez overthrew the Progressive General Espartero, whose campaign against the Carlist holdouts in 1840 had served both as the backdrop to Eugénie's summer adventure and as his road to power.

The girl queen was headstrong and promiscuous, and caused a great deal of trouble. When only ten she had been locked in a convent, but had escaped with a Polish man named Gorowsky. The pair were eventually discovered in Brussels.[105] Her contemporaries blamed her behaviour on the 1748 novel *Teresa the Philosopher* by Jean Baptiste Boyer. This book, a tale of a devout and beautiful young girl seduced by her Jesuit confessor was found in the Palace, and some of the courtiers believed it had been planted in the expectation that Isabella would read it, be led astray, and consequently 'pollute the throne'.[106]

Ignoring her voracious sexuality and having no concern for her own happiness, King Louis-Philippe of France arranged (through Bresson, his ambassador in Madrid) Isabella's marriage to Don Francisco de Asis, who was a known homosexual. Prince Albert wrote to his brother referring to Don Francisco as 'impotent' (a euphmism for homosexuality at that time) and 'half a fool'.[107] At the same time Louis-Philippe married his own son, the Duc de Montpensier, to Queen Isabella's sister Luisa Fernanda. Louis-Philippe's intention was that Isabella should have no children and as a consequence his own grandchild would succeed to the Spanish throne.[108]

Eugénie became a maid of honour, and her mother decided the time was right to bestow on her some of her father's titles. She became known as the Condesa de Teba, and was reported to have been heard storming around the palace shouting 'you must make him marry me', likely still in reference to Pepe. Their time at court was short-lived. Maria's dismissal followed a disagreement over precedence with the Master of the Queen's Household. Eugénie was probably not much improved by her exposure to Isabella's dissolute court.

In 1847 the Spanish writer Juan Valera (1824-1905) wrote to his mother telling of his invitation to a ball on 15th November to celebrate the day of Eugénie's patron saint. He described the 21-year-old Condesa as 'an infuriating girl, who with childish playfulness, shrieks, makes a noise, and gets up to all the naughtiness of a six-year-old child. At the same time she is quite the most fashionable young lady of this town and court, and she is so short-tempered and bossy, so fond of physical exercise and the flattery of good-looking gentlemen, and, in short so adorably badly brought up that one can be virtually certain that her future husband will be a martyr to this heavenly, aristocratic, and above all, wealthy creature.'[109] A news report in *El Heraldo* of June 1848 told of Eugénie, remarkably in the company of her beloved Pepe Alcañices, her sister Paca, and Paca's husband the Duque de Alba, riding together through the streets of Toledo dressed as smugglers.[110]

During the next few years Eugénie continued the social whirl of Europe, returning from time to time to Madrid where the de Montijos would catch up with their entertaining and the local social life. In May 1850 Eugénie was in Seville where her sister's family, the Albas, had a palace. The end of the month is the fiesta Cruces de Mayo, seemingly the reason for the visit. By 22th July she had moved on to Wiesbaden.

In 1851 the Great Exhibition took place in London. Although an enterprising company arranged a Cook's Tour from Spain, the de Montijo ladies decided to go as independent travellers – after all, they had ample entrée to the social life of London. On 21st June, Eugénie attended Lord Palmerston's party and on 13th July she and her mother were guests at a state ball at Buckingham Palace but were not amongst those privileged to be presented to Queen Victoria.[111]

From London they went on to Paris where Dr Thomas Evans (1823-1897), an American dentist, was in practice. In 1851 Eugénie visited Dr Evans professionally, accompanied as always by Pepa, who had been her maid since childhood.[112] She evidently found it easy to confide in him since he says he helped her to send gifts of money and presents 'saved from her own economies', secretly, to some poor Spanish emigrants in the United States. This may well have been a red herring. Generosity to strangers was out of character with Eugénie. More likely, the 'poor Spanish emigrants' referred to her child in England, who was by that time ten years old. A letter of Lord Clarendon's dated 15th October 1841, five months after Margaret's birth, states that he has just received two letters from Mrs Evans.[113] Was this Mrs Evans the Parisian dentist's wife, or perhaps code for Evans himself? Clarendon does seem to be in on the secret, whatever it is, by the time Eugénie visited England.

Dr Evans became a close friend and adviser of Eugénie and of Napoleon III. He brought up the eldest of Napoleon III's illegitimate sons, who was reputed to be the image of his father. (As James Michener reminds us, 'Any illegitimate daughters would have been placed in a convent — it was not possible to offer them as eligible brides, and marriage to an adventurer would have been a dangerous possibility.')[114] As Dr Hugenschmidt, this possible Bonaparte eventually took over Dr Evans' lucrative practice. Dr Evans escorted the Empress to the coast when she fled from Paris in 1870, and her friendship with him continued until his death in November 1897.[115]

* * *

Meanwhile in France, a February 1848 revolution had toppled King Louis-Philippe. In the December 1848 election that followed Prince Louis Napoleon, nephew of the great Napoleon Bonaparte, became President of the Republic. He was proclaimed Emperor of the French after mounting a *coup d'etat* on 2nd December 1851.

Now Napoleon III, he decided that he now needed a wife and a legitimate heir if he was to create a dynasty. A lifelong womaniser, his current mistress (who had already borne him two sons) was the English Elizabeth Howard (later Comtesse de Beauregard — the title was his 'farewell' gift). A very rich woman, she had lent her lover a large sum of money in his earlier days. Living conveniently close to the Palace in Paris, she followed the Emperor's suite around 'incognito', sometimes in a position of honour but never too obvious.

Louis Napoleon looked around at the available European princesses and through her parents approached Prinzessin Adelaide of Hohenlohe, a young niece of Queen Victoria. The Emperor of the French was a good catch and the girl was eager. The Queen, however, had heard of Louis Napoleon's reputation, and 'Ada' — very young and physically immature — was 'advised' to refuse him.

In the autumn of 1852 the court was, as usual in that season, at Compiègne, the 30,000-acre estate and hunting ground of the Kings of France. It was at Compiègne that the first Napoleon had met Marie Louise of Austria, and in this illustrious setting his successor, Napoleon III, fell for the charms of Eugénie de Montijo.

A house party at Compiègne was the first social function of the Imperial regime. Eugénie, who had been introduced to the Emperor by James de Rothschild, was a guest, and as was the custom was accompanied by her mother. Always in her element on the hunting field, she

Napoleon III, in a portrait from
1862 by Hippolyte Flandrin

flamboyantly exhibited her striking colouring and superb horsemanship, in contrast to her decorous and conventional turn-out when riding to hounds in England.

Disregarding the convention of the day she rode astride as she did as a child.[116] She wore a close-fitting riding jacket with her trousers covered by a roomy skirt. A diamond brooch held the large ostrich feather on her hat in place. Spurs decorated her high-heeled boots and she flourished a pearl-handled whip. Yet this spectacular woman resisted the advances of the Emperor: a new experience for him.

Eugénie's traumatic early love-life and her devotion to Pepe left her with no genuine interest in admirers, even the Emperor. Her rivals at court believed that she had told him that the only way to her bedroom lay through the chapel. They could not know that she was play-acting and hoping to make Pepe jealous. Although Louis Napoleon still awaited a reply to his proposition from Princess Ada, this exotic Spanish countess intrigued him.

An expert in the art of courtship, at the end of one day's hunting he presented Eugénie with the thoroughbred mount which had suited her well. The following morning he followed with a contrastingly simple yet romantic gesture — a bouquet of flowers. On an early morning walk in the woods Eugénie admired a clover leaf with dewdrops sparkling in the sun. Louis Napoleon never missed such a chance. Two days later he presented her with a brooch — a cloverleaf of emeralds with dewdrops of diamonds.

Maria had evidently kept her old lover Lord Clarendon in the picture. Their differences over his marriage forgotten, he arranged for Eugénie and Louis Napoleon to meet in secret in an apartment on the Champs Elysées. During these meetings the Emperor warned Eugénie of the dangers she would face if she were to become Empress. Clarendon reported this warning back to London, which improved Louis Napoleon's reputation in 'important places'.[117]

Eugénie was thinking along other lines. The offer of marriage from the Emperor was wonderful bait for the man she wanted, and she kept Louis Napoleon waiting for an answer.

Pepe de Alcañices, now Duke of Sexto, received her telegram: 'The Emperor has proposed, what am I to do?' The Secret Police intercepted the message and informed the Emperor. He apparently knew more about Eugénie than she realised; he told the police that he was perfectly aware of the situation and 'allowed the message to be delivered'.[118]

Pepe's reply read, 'Accept my heartiest congratulations.'[119]

The Emperor wanted to marry her, yet Pepe had still rejected her! She had asked Pepe, 'What am I to do?' and had once more been thrown back on her own resources. She had to decide for herself: if she was never to have Pepe, would life as an empress be such a bad alternative?

She decided to accept the Emperor's proposal, convincing herself that this role was predestined for her by divine Providence. She wrote in this vein to Queen Isabella of Spain before the public announcement of the engagement.

This was a marriage of convenience for both bride and groom. Afterwards Louis Napoleon told Lady Cowley, wife of the British Ambassador in Paris, that had he received an acceptance from Ada's father Prinz Hohenlohe, he would not have married Eugénie.[120]

The bride-to-be wrote to her sister on 15th January 1853, urging her to 'say nothing yet for fear of anonymous letters and tiresome things of that sort.' Her fears were not without foundation, in view of her hushed-up teenage affair and its tragic outcome. At the end of the month she wrote again to Paca, 'I have suffered a good deal in my life and had almost lost all hope of happiness.'[121]

Prosper Mérimée disapproved of her marriage, since he was only too aware that Eugénie's past left both her and the Emperor vunerable to blackmail. The old family friend wrote a number of letters to Madame de Montijo at this time.[122] Yet none of his letters written to her between 15th June 1852 and 5th February 1853 — the period between Eugénie's initial meeting with the Emperor and their marriage — are included in those which have been published. The first to appear is dated 29th April 1853. Evidently, Mérimée wrote very frankly of his concerns.

In 1941 the 17th Duque de Alba, Eugénie's great-nephew and Paca's grandson, told in his Oxford University lecture how the Empress read and destroyed these particular letters from Mérimée to her mother. 'We may regret this', he said, 'but according to her lofty ideals this was the only honourable thing to do'.[123]

The engagement of Eugénie, Condesa de Teba, to Napoleon III was announced on 16th January 1853. It came as no surprise in court circles. The ordinary citizens of Paris were not enthusiastic about their Emperor's choice. Neither, evidently, was Lord Cowley, the British Ambassador to France, 'an old and very intimate friend of the Emperor'.[124] He reported to Lord John Russell, the Prime Minister, as follows: 'She is I believe about six and twenty, very handsome, very coquette and (her success shews) very clever. Of course everyone now has some story against her, she has poisoned herself because her sister's husband would not consent to be her lover, *she has had a child* [italics mine]'.[125] This particular despatch has been retained in the Royal Archives at Windsor and is quoted by the Gracious Permission of her Majesty the Queen. Others from Cowley to Russell are preserved in the Public Records Office. A further report from Cowley to Russell, dated 20th January 1853, states: 'Things have been repeated to me which the Emperor has said of her, and others which have been said to him which it would be impossible to commit to paper'.[126]

King Leopold I of the Belgians wrote to Queen Victoria, passing on tales about Eugénie that had been told to him by the Infanta Isabel of Spain. According to the Infanta, Eugénie often wore the highly revealing Andalusian (lower-class) '*maja*' dress and had spent nights out in the open air near Madrid with young men 'where the chief fun was the sleeping arrangements'. Eugénie had worn a *maja* dress on a visit to Spa in 1849 when she was unchaperoned and in the company of several young men. In 1853 the *Illustrated London News* published a sketch of her wearing this dress. Indignant readers wrote to the paper protesting that she would never have worn such a garment since it was considered vulgar. Queen Victoria must have read Cowley's letter to Russell. She wrote to the Prinzessin of Prussia, 'The future Empress is beautiful, clever, and [quoting Cowley] "very coquette", passionate and wild'.[127] She said further that she did not believe that the scandals being circulated about Eugénie were true. A letter written by the Queen to King Leopold states that Lady Ely, her Lady of the Bedchamber, 'knows Mlle de Montijo quite well'.[128] The Marchioness of Ely had been Eugénie's chaperone during her time in England in 1851 and became her lifelong friend. She gave the Queen a more tolerant view of Eugénie's character and behaviour. Queen Victoria formed her own judgement and her diary entry for 20th January 1853 refers to the forthcoming marriage as 'the great news of the day'.

Paris was full of stories and vulgar songs about the

Emperor's bride. On the eve of the wedding, the newspapers published the story of the young Eugénie's 'attempted suicide'.[129] The Minister of the Interior, in a desperate attempt to stop the gossip, announced that people spreading rumours about the future Empress would be arrested. On 27th January the police actually took several people on the Rue de Bac into custody for what the press reported as being for the crime of 'lèse Montijo'.

The Elysée Palace had been prepared and set aside for the use of the de Montijo family, which proved to be only the bride and her mother. Her sister and brother-in-law remained in Spain. Their tardy excuse was that there was not enough time to travel to Paris.

The Queen of England sent Lady Augusta Bruce (later Lady Augusta Stanley), a lady-in-waiting to her mother the Duchess of York, to France. Victoria wanted a first-hand report. Lady Augusta's mother lived in Paris and her mother's close friend, Madame Mary Mohl (formerly Mary Clarke) was English, born in London. Mary Mohl was a staunch royalist and bitterly opposed to Napoleon III and his regime. These ladies were in the same social circle as Prosper Mérimée and Eugénie's aunt and uncle, the de Lesseps. Consequently Lady Augusta heard all the gossip and was able to pass it on to Queen Victoria.

Lady Augusta's letters, as edited by her nephew Albert Baillie, Dean of Windsor, were published in 1927. The book does not include any letters written at this particularly interesting time. In his notes, the Dean states that 'some, although interesting [to himself], are of no public concern'.

The houses in Nields
Row, the former home
of Robert and Abigail
Pemberton, and their
children Margaret,
Letitia and Sara

CHAPTER SIX

Margaret: Robert Starts Again

In January of 1839 Prince Louis Napoleon Bonaparte had visited Manchester, staying at Southport and at Bryn Hall, near Wigan. Manchester was full of cotton mills, their chimneys belching smoke that covered all of the buildings with a black veneer. The town was extremely prosperous and the main purpose of his visit was to see the new Stock Exchange. The Prince also visited various factories and the grand public edifices of the town, which was granted the status of a city some thirteen years later.

Robert Pemberton, who probably read of this visit, could never have dreamt how closely he would become involved with the Prince's family.

Robert and Abigail had become lovers, and they married on 11th July 1845.[130] In January 1846 at Barton-upon-Irewell Abigail gave birth to a daughter, Letitia Landon. Again tragedy struck: in June 1849, Letitia contracted pneumonia. The family had moved from Barton and were now living at number 7 Medlock Street, just around the corner from the main street, Deansgate, in central Manchester. After the three-year-old had been ill for just a week, Robert registered the death of yet another little daughter.

When the census was taken in March 1851 the Pembertons had moved to 18 Trumpet Street, off Deansgate.[131] Margaret, who evidently had a stronger constitution than her 'sisters', was listed as a nine-year-old scholar, born at Atherton. Although not quite ten years old she would have worked part-time in a cotton mill. At this time children were legally allowed to work for half a day provided they also attended school. Labour was at a premium in the expanding textile industry.

On 3rd June 1851, Abigail registered the birth of Letitia Elizabeth, signing with a cross. Her date of birth was given as the 5th of May, Eugénie's birthday. Two years later, on 27th June 1853, Sara Jane was born. Abigail registered this child just three days later on 30th June. By now they were living at 35 Ogden Street in Hulme, a little further away from the town centre.

It was the ambition of everyone in the overcrowded and unhealthy district of Manchester to move out of the town. The 1856 Manchester Directory gives Robert Pemberton's address as Leigh. In his old home district the air was cleaner and the overcrowding less of a problem. When their son Robert was born in 1861 just prior to the April census, the family had moved even further away from central Manchester, to Pennington.

The family now lived at 2 Nields Row, close to the church at Pennington. Robert continued his work as an overlooker of power looms. Abigail and Margaret worked as cotton weavers. The household included an elderly woman servant, Rachael Tickle, and the two younger daughters Letitia and Sara.

Robert's brother James lived further along the tidy terrace at No. 15. James's family included six sons and

their one daughter, also called Margaret. James's youngest son, born in 1860, was oddly named 'Doctor'. Perhaps
appropriately, he later became a schoolmaster.[132]

*The Empress Eugénie, after the painting
by Franz Xavier Winterhalter*

CHAPTER SEVEN

Eugénie: The Imperial Marriage

'[The Empress] is full of courage and spirits and yet so gentle, with such innocence and enjoyment that the ensemble is most charming. With all her great liveliness she has the prettiest and most modest manner.'
  – Queen Victoria, in her diary[133]

On the eve of her marriage Eugénie remarked pathetically, 'If Alcañices came to fetch me even today I would fly with him'.[134] In her biography of the Empress (written while Eugénie was still very much alive) Jane Stoddart quotes this remark made by 'one of the Empress's friends', commenting that 'it is an obvious invention'. From another perspective, it is instead an obvious sentiment.

The civil ceremony took place on the evening of 29th January 1853. The bride, who married under her title the Comtesse de Teba, wore a gown of white silk covered with Alençon lace and the diamond and sapphire belt that had belonged to Marie Louise. The ceremony was followed by a musical evening at the theatre attended by the entire wedding party.

When the new Empress returned to the Elysée Palace and was addressed as Majésté, the emotion of the day caught up with her and both the bride and her maid dissolved into nervous giggles. She then dashed off a hurried note to Paca, whose absence must have hurt her deeply. She told her sister that she felt as though she was acting in a play.

The following morning the religious ceremony took place in the great church of Notre Dame. Lush flowers and thousands of twinkling candles interspersed with multicoloured streamers filled the interior of the sanctuary. The pillars were draped with crimson and blue and capped with crowns and the intials 'E' and 'N'. A canopy of ermine-lined velvet covered the high altar in the centre of the church. State chairs for the bride and groom stood on a raised platform. People packed the cathedral. To the strains of the Wedding March the Emperor made his appearance with the bride already on his arm. She wore the Imperial Crown of Marie Louise and a wreath of orange blossoms from which fell a long veil. Her gown of white velvet was a splendid foil for the sparkling Regent diamond brooch. All was not perfect: horror of horrors, the ring had been forgotten! Princess Caroline Murat swiftly came to the rescue with the loan of her own. At the end of the ceremony the bride crossed herself before the altar, in the Spanish manner, using her thumb.

During the short drive back to the Tuileries Palace, the ornate crown on top of the wedding coach fell to the ground. This was considered to be very unlucky. It had happened before at the marriage of their ill-fated predecessors Napoleon and Marie Louise, whom he had married after his divorce from Josephine.

The Emperor's cousin Marie of Baden, who was

married to the Duke of Hamilton, was paired off with the Austrian Ambassador at the reception. She was in a raging temper and said, 'You will see the scandal I shall make when I get near my cousin'. The Ambassador was startled and quickly withdrew his arm telling her that she must walk alone. She then lost her nerve.[135] What scandal had she heard about? Had she heard of Eugénie's illegitimate daughter? Her husband, whilst still holding the title of Lord Douglas, had known Lord Cowley, the British Ambassador, before 1850.[136]

The waiting crowd of Parisians were not disappointed. The newly married couple appeared in all their splendour on the balcony of the Tuileries Palace before leaving for a formal dinner. From there, they departed for their honeymoon in the 'Villeneque de L'Etang' – the 'little house of the pool' – in the park of Saint-Cloud, in the countryside just outside Paris. The house still stands and is in use as a scientific establishment.

* * *

Eugénie enjoyed being an empress but evidently not a wife. Writing to a friend in the early days, she remarked that 'all cats are grey in the dark'. The pageantry of her role, such as reviewing the troops on horseback at the Emperor's side, appealed to her. By contrast, inside the palace she could relax and was seen by her staff charging around playing football with the footmen. Eugénie is said to have been obsessed with Queen Marie Antoinette. She would have been acutely conscious of her tragic predecessor who had lived in the very same rooms, slept in the same beds, and eaten and written at the same tables as herself in the royal palaces.

She wrote to her mother every day until Maria Manuela died in 1879. These letters, which would have been wonderful historical documents, have never been published. Her sister and brother-in-law also received regular letters from the Empress. The Spanish Embassy attended to the transmission of the correspondence.[137] The Albas were still not friendly towards her. On one occasion she wrote pathetically, 'I hope that you will write me a little affectionate word as I am upset by your unkind letter.'[138] Jacobo and Paca had made excuses not to go to their sister's marriage, and their replies to her correspondence in this period were always brief and curt.

It was not long before the Condesa de Montijo, mother of the new Empress, was persuaded to return to Spain. Lord Clarendon, her former lover, had encouraged her to go by telling her that in Spain she would be held in high esteem at the Court of Queen Isabella since she was now the mother of both the Duchess of Alba and the Empress of the French. Her old friend Prosper Mérimée escorted her for part of the journey.

In July 1853, the first year of her marriage, the new Empress and her mother both asked Mérimée to edit the Imperial Archives. In a letter to Honore Clair on 11th July 1853 he wrote, 'I have known the Empress for 25 years. Her mother was for me always the best loved friend that I have in the world. It is many months (since) her majesty offered me the place of director of archives.' He goes on to quote her stating that if he did not accept he would be their enemy. His reply to Eugénie had been that he did not have the talent or the 'gout'.[139]

Mérimée wrote to his friend Leon Laborde from Madrid in November of that year – he was evidently staying with the Empress's mother – saying towards the end of a long letter, 'I am very pleased that you speak to me about the archives. It appears that the Empress has written the same thing to her mother', giving no hint as to what Laborde had said.[140]

Although the Emperor and Empress had this 'fine position' ready for Mérimée, he had other ideas, being more interested in his studies of ancient monuments 'That,' Fleury quotes Mérimée saying, 'is how I came to lose my liberty'.[141]

In 1853 Mérimée wrote to friends saying that he wished he could adopt a little girl, a rather strange notion for a middle-aged man. Did he have a particular little girl in mind?[142]

On 2 August 1853, Mérimée wrote a cryptic letter to Madame Delessert, telling her that Madame de Montijo had written to him about 'rather bad matters' at her house and had asked him to 'make a little announcement concerning 1840.'[143] (Should any doubt remain, this letter is strong evidence that Eugénie's friends and family were actively covering up the events of that year.) Inevitably Maria would always have been worried about the occurrences of 1840, and there was currently a great deal of gossip about the new Empress.

What was this 'little announcement' Mérimée was being asked to make? Could it have been a contrived alibi for that particular period, such as an embroidery of the 'suicide attempt' story? None of the letters that he wrote to Madame de Montijo during this period — from the time of her daughter's first meeting with the Emperor until after this first year of her marriage — have emerged. According to Eugénie's great-nephew the 17th Duque de Alba, the Empress had burned them herself, which is certainly likely.

On 10th May 1854, the year following the marriage, Mérimée wrote yet another cryptic message in a letter to Madame de Montijo. He told her that he had received a mysterious box from an unknown address. He referred to the handwriting, which he said reminded him of some impertinent letters and an anonymous correspondent.

Had 'Madame X', who had taken the infant to England, reappeared?

The imperial marriage was one of convenience for both the Emperor and Eugénie. He needed a legitimate heir and she had reluctantly come to terms with what was, to her, second best. Her dutiful pregnancy was not to be easy; there were two miscarriages in the early days of her marriage, possibly the result of lasting damage from her early teenage childbirth.

During these early days, prior to her 1855 state visit to Queen Victoria, the Empress visited England several times, incognito and without the Emperor. The staff at the Tuileries Palace were told that she was visiting relatives in Scotland. This was not so. Under the name of Madame Guzman, she stayed at a house at Watford owned by a Mr Coleman 'who knew perfectly well who she was'. His house was close to 'The Grove', the Watford home of Lord Clarendon, her mother's former lover, and Clarendon visited her daily.[144]

In Paris, Eugénie's daily life as Empress varied widely. Visits to the theatre were very much part of the lively social scene of the Second Empire during this, the era of Offenbach. When the Empress saw Meilhac and Halevy's play *Frou-Frou* in 1868, it was reported that she was obviously very upset.[145] *Frou-Frou* was the story of a woman escaping from a dull marriage and going away to Venice with her lover. Evidently she empathised with the heroine.

The extravagant lifestyle of the court has attracted most of the attention, but Eugénie involved herself in many good works, patronising an orphanage in the city that cared for 300 girls and trained them for future employment.[146] She visited hospitals, slums and prisons, going about in an unmarked landau accompanied by her coachman dressed anonymously in black livery.[147] She

80

founded the Eugénie and Napoleon Home, where 'inmates were given a small dowry to enable them to marry or to take up a business of their own choosing.'[148] In addition, politics were now beginning to interest her and despite her inexperience she began to influence her evidently gullible husband in his decision-making.

* * *

In the spring of 1855 Queen Victoria and Prince Albert invited Napoleon III and his Empress to visit England. Lords Clarendon and Granville had arranged the visit, a formal state occasion, for diplomatic reasons.[149] The Emperor and Empress spent three nights in Windsor and two in London.

Initially Queen Victoria regarded entertaining her French guests as a duty. Happily the two couples got along famously and greatly enjoyed themselves. Personal appearance was important to the Queen. Her journal entry for 17th April 1855 refers to Eugénie: 'She is v pleasing v graceful and v unaffected but v delicate. She is certainly v pretty and v uncommon looking'.[150] On 19th April the Queen wrote, 'been entirely occupied with our Imperial guests with whom I am v much pleased and who behave really with the greatest tact.'

Victoria was quite smitten with the Emperor. Being of similar rank to herself he had made the most of his opportunity and used his well-practised charms, even flirting with her. The dancing in the evenings was a special treat for the two elder children of Victoria and Albert, the Prince of Wales and the Princess Royal, known familiarly as Bertie and Vicky. Eugénie was very popular with them both. Princess Vicky was the same age as her own secret child, who surely would be in her thoughts. Of necessity, when business had to take over, political discussions were arranged between the Queen and the Emperor. Lords Palmerston and Clarendon were both present at these meetings.

When the time came for the visitors to return home there were tearful goodbyes all round. The Emperor invited his hosts to visit him in France, and lost no time in making the arrangements. After landing at Boulogne where she was met by the Emperor, on 18th August 1855 the reigning sovereign of Great Britain set foot in Paris, the first to do so since the coronation of Henry VI in 1431.

Bertie and Vicky accompanied Queen Victoria and Prince Albert. Lord Clarendon was included in the party and did not miss the opportunity of visiting his former mistress, Madame de Montijo, who was conveniently in Paris at the same time. Eugénie was in the early days of her pregnancy. The Emperor was able to entertain Queen Victoria, but the Empress's frequent rest periods left poor Prince Albert rather to his own devices.

The royal family stayed at the Emperor's summer palace, Saint-Cloud, which stood on a hillside across the Seine opposite the Bois de Boulogne. In the gardens the waterfalls, cascades, and fountains were a delight, particularly in the heat of summer. Queen Victoria, always troubled by hot weather, wrote to King Leopold from Paris, saying, 'The heat is very great, but the weather splendid, and though the sun may be hotter, the air is certainly lighter than ours — and I have no headache'.[151]

The royal guests were taken to see the Louvre, the Tuileries Palace and the Palace of Versailles, to be feted with a State Ball in the fabulous Hall of Mirrors. The visit, which lasted nine days, proved very popular with the Parisians. They decorated their streets and turned out in large numbers whenever the English royals appeared in public.

What must the populace have thought of Queen Victoria's wardrobe? On her arrival in the city she was reported to have been wearing a white flounced dress and black slippers, criss-crossed with black ribbons. She carried a bright green sunshade with a matching mantle, and a large bag decorated with an embroidered gilt poodle, a home-made gift from one of her children. Yet her regal manner and bearing, particularly noticeable on her visit to the opera, outshone her fashionably dressed hostess, and it was the Queen who stole the show and gained the admiration of the Parisians.

The young English prince and princess adored Paris and also their imperial hosts. They evidently told the Empress that they did not want to go home, since she told them that they could not stay on as their parents would miss them. The Prince of Wales retorted that he thought not since there were plenty more children at home!

Eugénie felt sorry for the young Princess Victoria, whose wardrobe left much to be desired. After her return to England Vicky was delighted to receive a charming and tactful present from her hostess in Paris: a lifesize doll built exactly to her own measurements and dressed in the very latest Paris fashion. As the Empress had intended, her young friend undressed the doll and wore the clothes herself. Eugénie now had an admirer for life. The Emperor was currently likewise in Queen Victoria's good books; she wrote to her Uncle Leopold on 20th August 1855 to say, 'I have formed a great affection for the Emperor'.[152]

Lord Clarendon, 'Queen Victoria's erstwhile favourite',[153] was always on friendly terms with the Emperor and Empress. He dined at the Tuileries on 17th February 1856, the day after the birth of the Prince Imperial. On 11th February Katherine, Lady Clarendon, had written to her husband's sister from the Hotel du Louvre saying

83

that she expected to have her audience with the 'Em-prejo' the following day.[154] Clarendon visited Compiègne on the Emperor's invitation in November 1858, and the imperial couple entertained him on many other recorded occasions.

CHAPTER EIGHT

Margaret: Enter James

Pennington was in farming country, and amongst the many land workers was James Cartlidge. Born in 1837, he was the fifth son of Samuel Cartlidge. Samuel was well known in the village of Astbury, over the county border in Cheshire. The Cartlidges had been associated with Astbury's magnificent and renowned church for many generations. Samuel, James's father, was for seven years the local schoolmaster and for a remarkable seventy the parish clerk. His neat and well-formed handwriting in the immaculate registers makes the reason for his long service apparent.

Samuel married twice and had sixteen surviving children. In July 1855 Hannah (*née* Painter), his wife, died. The next month, his fourth (but eldest surviving) son, also named Samuel, a sergeant in the 91st Regiment of Foot, died of disease in the Crimean War. That same year Samuel Cartlidge married again, a young local girl named Sarah Ann Shufflebotham. Perhaps in response James, who worked in the Congleton silk mill, left his father's house.

Astbury farmer David Brindley of Peel Farm had relatives at Leigh where James, who evidently preferred the open air, went to work on a farm.

The Leigh Parish Church had a Scottish vicar, Irvine by name, who was not popular with the congregation having tried, amongst other things, to socialise the church by breaking down family pews. The parishioners were not able to get rid of him, and so built a new church close by at Pennington. There James likely met Margaret Pemberton, who lived in Nield's Row, Pennington, and worked in the local cotton mill.

The petite Margaret might have been the subject of romantic whispers that she was not the natural child of her parents but was Spanish and the daughter of a great lady. Perhaps she had inherited her mother's looks, and thereby captivated James. She certainly inherited her mother's free-wheeling approach to family planning. In July 1859, when she was eighteen years old, Margaret became pregnant. Three months later, on 16th October 1859, she married James Cartlidge a farm labourer in Pennington church. Margaret's trade was given as 'weaver'. Joseph Pemberton and Mary Fazakerley were the witnesses.

CHAPTER NINE

Eugénie: The Dynasty is Assured

The Prince Imperial, heir to Napoleon III, had been born on Sunday 16th March 1856 after a very difficult labour lasting many hours. The baby was named Eugéne Louis Bonaparte et Guzman and baptised on the day of his birth, the custom of the Roman Catholic Church. His grandmother the Comtesse de Montijo placed a gold chain and medallion around his neck.[155]

The Emperor was delighted to have a legitimate son and heir, although he was told that his wife's physical condition was such that she must have no more children. He, as always, had mistresses, so this news was no hardship for him, nor apparently was it for his wife.

In April 1857, the year following the birth of her son, Eugénie paid a private visit to the Duke and Duchess of Hamilton at their palace just outside Glasgow.

On 5th May 1857, Prince Albert opened an important art exhibition at Trafford Park in Manchester. Eugénie may well have visited her child in Manchester under cover of this exhibition on her way back to London. Her letters

The Emperor Napoleon, the Empress
Eugénie and the Prince Imperial

of that period which have been published are without addresses but dated 9th April, 2nd May, and 3rd May. The next letter is dated 31st December 1857. The consistent lack of documentation at interesting times seems more than coincidental.

Prosper Mérimée wrote to Madame de Montijo from Paris on 7th June 1857, 'I leave tomorrow for London with M. and Mme. Fould [Minister of State and of Finance] … perhaps I will take a little excursion.'[156] Achille Fould's position during the first eight years of the Second Empire was held to be very important. Fould had a hand in 'suggesting and arranging everything and the Emperor was in his hands.'[157] On 30th June, Mérimeé wrote to a friend, 'I am moderately charmed with Manchester.'[158] He had visited the art exhibition and wrote an article about it for *Le Moniteur*, which was published on 9th July 1857.

A letter to Madame de Montijo from Paris dated 13 July tells that he has returned from Manchester, which he found 'very handsome' and continues, cryptically as ever, 'perhaps one would have been able to see better without having to search for it so far.'[159] What was he searching for? Both Manchester and the art exhibition would have been easy to find. Was he looking for something or someone else in the district? Had he been asked to look into the welfare of Eugénie's daughter?

A conscientious mother, Eugénie was in many respects very hard on her son. She had been strictly brought up herself in her father's lifetime, and perhaps knew only too well what could happen if an aristocratic child was coddled.

Politics now began to interest her, as she knew that the life of her son would be affected by the future of the Empire. The Emperor was now suffering intermittent but excruciating pain caused by kidney stones. His illness likely allowed the Empress to have more influence on his decision making than would have been the case had he been fit and well.

The British royal and French imperial couples had an increasingly cordial relationship. The Emperor and Empress privately visited Queen Victoria at Osborne House on the Isle of Wight on 6th August 1857.[160] In August of the following year the Queen was the guest of the Emperor on board the *Bretagne* when the imperial couple were with the French fleet at Cherbourg.

* * *

Although Eugénie still carried her torch for her beloved Pepe, and remarkably even hosted him as a guest of herself and the Emperor, his attentions were elsewhere. He allegedly carried on an affair with the promiscuous Queen Isabella II of Spain. By this time no further censure attached to Isabella's conduct, and she even attracted some sympathy. Years earlier, on 9th December 1849, Queen Victoria had written in her journal, 'Queen Isabella having divested herself of the odious husband nevertheless became officially enceinte (for the first time) at the end of 1849,' continuing, 'It is a very good thing and no one will be inclined to cavil as to who was *the real father*, considering her very peculiar and distressing marriage – For which *she*, poor creature, is in no wise to blame....'[161] [Emphasis in original.]

Her affair with Pepe must have culminated in February of 1857, as Alfonso (later to be King Alfonso XII of Spain), who was believed to be Pepe's son, was born in November of that year. Louis, the Prince Imperial, and Prince Alfonso became playmates.[162]

No letters of Eugénie's have been published dated after July 1856, implying that Pepe's love affair with Isabella began around then.

Like the Spanish court, the French court was full of love affairs and intrigue. Gossips whispered that the Emperor was actually the son of a Dutch admiral or the chancellor René de Villeneuve and not of Louis Bonaparte.[163] His mother, Queen Hortense of the Netherlands, was not entirely faithful, after all. The Emperor had an illegitimate half-brother, the Duc de Morny, whose father was the Comte de Flahaut. As Vizetelly tells it, 'his birth was falsely registered and Hortense paid the "father" £240 annually, after the "father's" death he was entrusted to Madame de Souza in London.'[164] Competition flared in the court between the Emperor's half brother Morny, and Comte Walewski, one of Napoleon I's illegitimate sons, both wishing to have precedence.

Whilst in St Petersburg when French Ambassador in 1856, Morny married a Russian woman, Sophie Troubetzkoi. She was half his age and had been lady-in-waiting to the Tsarina. Sophie had no money but was supposedly given an 'important' dowry by the Tsar.

After Morny died in March 1865, the Empress ordered all his papers confiscated, including his private papers and secret documents. His widow Sophie was furious but was powerless to do anything about it.

The following year Eugénie wrote to her mother saying that she hoped Pepe had not run into any kind of danger. Was this danger the widowed Sophie? She was by now a very rich woman, and she had an 'evil' temper.[165] If Sophie had deliberately set out to attract Pepe in order to get her own back on the Empress she was certainly successful. Pepe and Sophie married in the spring of 1868.[166]

In the by now familiar pattern, there are no published letters of Eugénie written at the time of Pepe's marriage in 1868.

James and Margaret
Cartlidge with their sons
Albert and James Robert
Samuel (date unknown)

CHAPTER TEN

Margaret: A Son in Lancashire

On 16th April 1860, six months after her wedding, Margaret bore a son, to be named Albert. The child was born at Robert Pemberton's house [the certificate is wrongly recorded as Cartridge], given as as it was the custom of the time for a girl to go home for the birth of her first child. The baby was not given a family name, unusual in the Cartlidge family for the firstborn, but judging by Albert's features when grown up there is no reason to question his paternity.

Margaret registered the birth herself. She did not sign his birth certificate although she had signed her marriage certificate. Subsequently she signed some, but not all of the birth certificates of her very large family. This inconsistency was not unusual at the time. Registrars appear to have assumed that most women were illiterate and requested them to 'make your mark here'. Probably it was less tiresome to conform than to protest.

CHAPTER ELEVEN

Eugénie: I Must Go To Manchester

'I was informed some days ago confidentially that the Empress was about to make a tour in Scotland, but as I could hardly believe it I did not write to you upon the subject. It seems however that it is perfectly true and she sets out tomorrow morning. I am told that she has written to the Queen explaining that she guards the strictest incognito and that she wishes no notice to be taken of her. Various motives are attributed to this somewhat extraordinary proceeding – grief, ill health, jealousy.... I leave you to put your own construction on the journey, which I believe is not to be prolonged beyond a fortnight.'
  – letter of Lord Cowley, British Ambassador in Paris, to Prime Minister Lord John Russell, 13th November 1860[167]

By the spring of 1860 the Duque and Duquesa of Alba, Eugénie's sister and brother-in-law, were more kindly disposed towards their sister. They moved into a splendid house on the Champs Élysées that she had built for them. A house-warming fancy-dress ball described as 'extravagant and outrageous' took place. Whatever Eugénie's motives were in building the house and her sister's in accepting the new arrangement became moot, as their reconciliation was to be tragically cut short. Paca suffered from breast cancer, but the doctors told Eugénie that her sister was not in any immediate danger. They may not have been aware that the cancer had spread to her spine.

Reassured, the Emperor and Empress spent the summer at their favourite home, Saint-Cloud, followed by a state visit to the south of France prior to travelling on to Corsica and the French colony of Algeria, where they arrived on 17th September 1860.

Paca had died on 16th September, the day before. The courtiers withheld this tragic news from her sister until three days later, when Eugénie was aboard the royal yacht on her way back to France. She arrived in Paris angry and inconsolable. She was too late even for the funeral, which had been held at the Church of the Madeleine the previous day. She had not been convinced by the doctors' prognosis, telling the Comtesse Stephanie de Tascher that she had been in constant fear on the journey and during the stay in Algeria.

Jane Stoddart says of this period, 'Now that [Paca] was dead, the sense of loneliness was almost more than [Eugénie's] expansive nature could bear.'[168] Yet on 23rd October Mérimée lunched with the Imperial family and reported that he found Eugénie 'full of enthusiasm over her visit to Corsica'. Her dramatic mood swings at the time of her bereavement were to be repeated in later life when her illegitimate daughter died. At this time, however, her good mood might have been due to a newfound resolution: to finally meet her daughter.

* * *

If Eugénie now knew what she was doing and why, she was almost the only one. Her sudden departure in November 1860 for Britain mystified French society. The Parisians were led to believe that she was visiting her Scottish relatives. She certainly spent a few days visiting her husband's cousin the Duchess of Hamilton, but there is no evidence to suggest that she ever visited any of her mother's relatives, the Kirkpatricks. According to Dame Ethel Smyth, Eugénie 'gloried in her illustrious Spanish descent but was not happy about the other side [of her family]'.[169] Stoddart refers to the rumours swirling about Eugénie's trip, and hints at the confusion she left behind: 'One of these was that Eugénie was jealous of the attentions which Napoleon was paying to a lady of the Court; but if that were the cause the poor Empress might very often have set forth upon solitary wanderings.'[170]

Even Mérimée expressed ignorance, writing in November 1860 to his old friend the Italian Chief Librarian of the British Museum, Sir Anthony Panizzi, who he had first met in 1840, Eugénie's year of mystery: 'Here is some odd news between you and me.'[171] To Madame de Montijo, Mérimée wrote that 'her marred judgment is guessed as the reason for the voyage of the Empress. In Scotland in November! You can guess all the foolishness which she has spoken on this occasion. It is always bad to repeat the speculation and idle words. I believe that S.M. [Sa Majésté] after the two months of very sad retreat which have passed, feels the need of a little succour.'[172] To his close friend Jenny Dacquin he wrote: 'The voyage of the Empress is causing much talk and nobody understands anything.'[173] Madame Baroche said, 'even though the voyage is a sort of mystery it is not good taste to penetrate.'[174] As Mérimée observed to Maria, Scotland is not by any standard the ideal place to choose for a holiday in the short, dark and dreary days of November. Eugénie loved the sun; during her exile she left England each winter for her villa at Cap Martin in the south of France.

Her putative English hosts and their correspondents were no more enlightened. A letter dated 22nd November 1860 to Queen Victoria from King Leopold I of the Belgians reads: '...Scotland for an excursion in winter. I believe that the death of her sister has affected her a great deal, the Queen was shocked that Eugénie had danced in Africa whilst her poor sister was dying.'[175] (A most unfair criticism since the Empress did not know of her beloved sister's decline.) David Duff writes that Queen Victoria, puzzled as everyone else, set her 'ever vigilant spy' Lady Augusta Bruce on the trail.[176] One published letter from Lady Augusta, dated 22nd November 1860 from Frogmore, reads: 'You will see by the papers what an escapade the Empress had made — The mystery in which her proceedings were tried to be shrouded in Paris made people say thousands of things.'[177]

Queen Victoria wrote to her daughter on 17th November, 'Then imagine your favourite Empress has arrived suddenly in England, quite incognito and goes on today to Hamilton Palace in Scotland.' (Lady Hamilton was Princess Marie of Baden, the Emperor's cousin who had threatened to 'make a scandal' at the wedding.) 'She has written to me herself and we hear the same from Paris — that her health and nerves are so shaken by the death of her sister that a journey is absolutely necessary but that on her return she hoped to see me ... it is very extraordinary.'[178] To her uncle King Leopold I, Victoria wrote, 'it is altogether very strange.' Prince Albert referred to the Scottish journey when writing to his Prussian in-laws: 'The secret history of her visit is unknown to us, I will not bore you with mere guesses, thousands are in circulation.'[179]

Later writers seem similarly baffled, or perhaps silenced. The Comte de Fleury's two-volume *Memoirs of the Empress Eugénie* is the most comprehensive biography of the imperial couple. Published in 1920, the year the Empress died, the biography's title is remarkable since in her will Eugénie instructs her solicitors to take action if anything purporting to be her memoirs was published. The writer's father General Fleury had been a member of the Emperor's Presidential household, his aide-de-camp, and had been the French Consul in Liverpool during the Empress's 1860 jaunt. The Comte had been a playmate of the Prince Imperial and appears to have had intimate knowledge of the affairs of the Second Empire. And yet, when referring to the year 1860 Fleury makes *no mention* of the Scottish journey! He comments (incorrectly) later in the book that the Empress's journey in 1864 to Schwalbach in Germany was the first time that she had travelled under the name of 'Comtesse de Pierrefonds', hoping that she would not be recognised.[180] Even modern historians seem to have missed the extra three days she spent in Manchester. David Duff, author of *Eugénie and Napoleon III*, had noticed that the journey from Scotland left a few days unaccounted for, although his time-scale was not quite right. 'She received an Address at Manchester, was mobbed at Leamington and then disappeared for a while. She surfaced at Claridges on 2nd. December.'[181]

Lord Clarendon, who almost alone appears to have known what was going on, remarked, 'Her journey seems to me to have its share of a certain "timidité" which will be [a] new experience for her'.[182]

Eugénie departed for Britain on 14th November 1860. The Empress travelled under the name of the Comtesse de Pierrefonds, accompanied by two ladies of the court, the Comtesse de Montébello and Madame Souliez, and two gentlemen, Monsieur de la Grange and Colonel Pavé. We at least have the historical record as transmitted by Jane Stoddart: 'On Wednesday 14th November, Napoleon saw the "Countess of Pierrefonds" away from the Gare du

Nord. The government papers had received orders not to write about her departure.'[183]

* * *

The Empress arrived late in London on 14th November and stayed overnight at the then very ordinary Claridges Hotel. The following day she walked around the shops in the morning and in the afternoon visited the Crystal Palace. According to Lord Malmesbury, her doings caused surprise and displeasure to the English who had spoken to him on the subject.[184]

On 17th November she arrived in Edinburgh, where she received an address from the Town Council. She replied in English. She had a consultation with Dr James Simpson, an eminent gynaecologist. The gossips found out and assumed that she was worried that, like her sister, she had cancer. It was likely more innocuous: one of her ladies has recorded that Eugénie regularly suffered from incapacitating menstrual pain.[185]

From Edinburgh she travelled to Killiecrankie and Stirling in very wintry weather, then to Perth and Glasgow before arriving at nearby Hamilton Palace in Motherwell at the end of the month. Her alias was not effective; wherever she went there were crowds waiting to see her.

Lord Lamington, a fellow guest at Hamilton Palace, said that 'the Empress talked very little and afterwards with her entourage it was impossible to gain any information. In fact there was an air of profound mystery over the whole proceeding.'[186] A footnote to the page states, 'Lord Lamington adds that a friend wrote to him offering to tell him the two most confidential secrets entrusted to him lately, in exchange for that of the Empress's journey; but that, as far as he was concerned, the secret was

Eugénie's November 1860 Journey

13 Nov	The Empress Eugénie leaves St-Cloud.
14 Nov	Arrives London. First to Claridges, then a morning's shopping, followed by a visit to the Crystal Palace in the afternoon (Anna Bicknell).
16 Nov	Leaves London. Overnight stop in York. (Duff, p. 148)
17 Nov	Leaves York for Edinburgh, Douglas Hotel (*The Scotsman*). Visits Holyrood Palace, calls on Dr Simpson, explored Melrose, Abbotsford and Dalkeith.
23 Nov	Reached Birnam Hotel at Dunkeld. Visited Perth, Stirling and Taymouth Castle via Lochs Katrine and Lomond, to Glasgow and thence to Hamilton Palace, Glasgow.
29 Nov	Leaves Hamilton, arrives Manchester, Queen's Hotel (*Manchester Examiner and Times*). Visits a cotton mill.
30 Nov	Drives around various locations in Manchester.
1 Dec	Leaves Manchester and arrives Leamington Spa, Regent Hotel.
2 Dec	Cuts short expected stay of two to three days. Leaves for London in the early afternoon.
3 Dec	In London. Writes to brother-in-law Duque de Alba.
4 Dec	Windsor. Lunch with Queen Victoria and Prince Albert.
5-8 Dec	London, Claridges Hotel. Called on Panizzi at British Museum, shown over new Reading Room (date uncertain). Spent two hours at Tussauds.
9 Dec	At Stafford (now Lancaster) House as guest of Duke and Duchess of Sutherland.
11 Dec	London, at Claridges, visited by Queen Victoria.
12 Dec	London. In the evening escorted by Mr Claridge to the station.
13 Dec	Sailed from Folkestone to Boulogne, met by the Emperor at Amiens.
19 Dec	Flauhault writes on the Empress's behalf to the mayor of Manchester.
20 Dec	In Paris.

like the knife-grinder's story — there was none to tell.' No evidence has come to light to ascertain whether the Duke of Hamilton and his wife knew the reason for their guest's visit.

The Empress or one of her entourage, having realised that her disguise was not effective, attempted to divert attention from her true destination. It was given out that when she left Hamilton Palace she would be travelling to Liverpool where a suite of rooms had been booked for her at the Adelphi Hotel by General Fleury, the French Consul. However, at the last minute she 'changed her mind', deciding not to visit Liverpool after all, 'but thought it desirable to pay a visit to Manchester', according to the report the Manchester *Examiner and Times* published on 30th November 1860 from its Liverpool correspondent. Her desire was more urgent than the *Examiner and Times* implied. At the end of November 1860, Eugénie wrote her brother-in-law, saying, 'I hope that you will write me a little affectionate word as I am upset by your unkind letter,' ending, 'Goodbye my dear James, I must go to Manchester.'[187]

Liverpool is about 23 miles from Leigh, where James and Margaret lived. Central Manchester is 10 miles nearer to Leigh. The centre of the cotton industry, Manchester was granted the status of a city in 1853. In the central area there were new warehouses with imposing palatial facades. Behind them stood the cotton mills and appalling slum dwellings. Building land was sold on very short lease, and consequently speculators threw up more houses of the lowest possible standard for a quick return from the rents paid by the rush of people moving into the city for work.

Manchester must have come as a shock for the agricultural labourers. The smoke from the factory chimneys was so dense that it was only possible to see clearly on

Sundays when the factories were closed. The polluted rivers and canals smelled appallingly. When Queen Victoria made a visit, quicklime had to be poured into the waters in a frantic attempt to overcome the stench. As recently as 27th August 1995 *The Times* stated that Manchester was the fourth most depressing place on earth, with a quarter of the citizens suffering from nervous conditions.[188] The city has since been changed beyond recognition, and hosted the Commonwealth Games 2002.

In November 1860, however, Eugénie did not see Manchester to great advantage. The weather at the time was November at its very worst. A local diarist, John O'Neile of Clitheroe, wrote of those very days (29th November through 1st December 1860) that they were 'the darkest he had ever known and that lights were burned all day'.[189]

The Empress arrived at Manchester Victoria Station on Thursday 29th November and drove in a carriage to the the Queen's Hotel, where she stayed until noon on 1st December. 'Her arrival took the inhabitants entirely by surprise... at 5 p.m. the Mayor and his daughter were ushered into the august presence, he observed that only having heard of the intended visit late on the previous evening...'[190] She had no official engagements in the city.

Despite the lack of formal publicity, the Manchester *Examiner and Times* reported the Empress's visit in detail and at great length. One of the first places she visited was a cotton-weaving shed at the mill of Sir Elkanah Armitage and Sons at Pendleton. In the weaving shed she took a deep interest in what she saw and asked many questions despite the great noise. She then visited a public library and attempted unsucessfully to visit a shooting range. (This might appear strange, but Prosper Mérimée had taught her to shoot as a child in 1837.) She abandoned the visit because her carriage was too wide to pass through the tollhouse gate. She visited the Macintosh rubber works, a silk warehouse, and Peel Park where she saw a statue of the Queen; and she received, presumably at her hotel, an address from the local council. The newspaper stated that 'it was believed that the Empress had entertained the local Mayor to dinner one evening'. She did not, as there is no record, official or otherwise, of any such invitation. She dined, rather, behind drawn blinds. The crowds, not used to illustrious lady visitors, hung about after dark, looking up at the windows hoping to get a glimpse of her.

Empress Eugénie and her entourage left Manchester London Road Station on 1st December. The *Examiner and Times* reported on 3rd December 1860 that on leaving her Majesty said that she 'had been very very comfortable and was pleased and very happy'. An interesting comment for a woman in mourning, and one who had travelled directly to Manchester from a palace standing in a large park. At home in France she had the palaces of the Tuileries, Compiègne, Fontainbleu, Saint-Cloud and Versailles at her disposal, in addition to smaller houses such as Villa Eugénie at Biarritz. She had often been a guest in the royal palaces of England and Spain.

It cannot have been the appalling working and living conditions of Manchester, seen and smelled at their very worst in the gloom of November, which had made her so 'very, very comfortable, pleased and very happy'. Her pleasure and happiness would have been in the meeting for which her entire tour had provided cover: a rendezvous in Manchester with her long-lost daughter, who by now had a husband and a baby son.

The press recorded her journey on to Leamington in the minute detail customary at the time. The report included the detail of the Duke and Duchess of Sutherland with their son and daughter joining the train at Trentham. It was an unplanned but most cordial meeting according to the report in the newspaper. The *Royal Leamington Spa Courier and Warwickshire Standard* reported '[The Empress] arrived at 4 p.m. on Saturday [1st December]', and that she 'was smiling'. A further dispatch from that organ reads that Eugénie was 'completely recruited after the fatigues incidental to her long journey of the previous day ... the Empress attended [Sunday 2nd December] the 11 o'clock service at the Roman Catholic Church. After the service the Rev. J. Jeffries ascended the pulpit, and delivered a brief but exceedingly able and impressive discourse on the subject of the Last Judgement. On retiring from the Chapel the Empress entered her carriage and drove to the Regent Hotel. Her Majesty, we regret to state, looked very pale and careworn.'

Rev. Jeffries' sermon had alarmed and distressed Eugénie. Memories of her early love affair and the resulting concealed illegitimate child could account for her abrupt change of mood that Sunday. Her loyalty to the Roman Catholic Church may have changed afterwards. In a letter to her daughter in 1879, some years later, Queen Victoria commented, 'I seldom saw anyone less priest-ridden than she was and is…. She never goes to Mass but on a Sunday (excepting on v. exceptional occasions). The English RCs have hardly been civil to her. So much for that.'[191]

The *Courier and Warwickshire Standard* continued its comprehensive coverage: 'It was fully expected that the Empress would have remained at Leamington until Monday or Tuesday; but on Saturday a telegraphic message was received which it is understood hastened her departure…. At 2.35 p.m. on Sunday Dec. 2nd, the Station Master was informed that the Empress would be leaving for London on the 2.56 p.m. train. Mr Fryer had arranged for a Saloon carriage to be sent from London for the return journey, it had not yet arrived and so he hurredly organised an ordinary first class coach as a substitute.'[192]

The next day, 3rd December 1860, Eugénie wrote from London to her brother-in-law Alba, 'My health is better and I hope that my return to Paris will not be too sad for I wish to wrestle with my pain. I embrace you tenderly.'[193] (Vizetelly reports, 'To none of those who saw her during her tour in Scotland did she appear to be at all ailing.')[194] Out of context she includes a cryptic remark: 'Do you not find one requests too much of children.'

Was her request secrecy forever about their relationship from her daughter and son-in-law? Or perhaps her comment was a rueful acknowledgement that her expectations for the Manchester visit had been too ambitious.

On 4th December the Empress, still in an emotional state, went to lunch with Queen Victoria and Prince Albert at Windsor Castle. The next day the Queen wrote to her daughter, 'The poor Empress came yesterday – no demonstrations beyond Papa's going down to the station to bring her up and our all being at the door to receive her. She was in dark mourning – lovely and charming – but so sad! She cried in speaking of her shattered nerves – (she could neither eat nor sleep till she came here) … I fear there is some great sorrow preying upon her.'[195]

A letter dated 5th December 1860 from Lord Clarendon to the Duchess of Manchester reads: 'What an odd little visit the Empress seems to have paid the Q – hardly time enough to get some luncheon and see the Dss. of Kent. As Puss was there you will probaby have heard all about it so please tell me whenever you are charitably disposed to write.'[196]

On 9th December Eugénie was staying at Stafford, now called Lancaster House, with the Duchess of Sutherland. Lord Clarendon had been invited but in a letter dated 10th December he said that he had received the Duchess's invitation too late for the Sunday trains and commented, 'I daresay it went off less stiffly than at Windsor wh: latter affair does not seem to have left a very favorable impression of the Eugenian mind. I am sure The Q INTENDED to be civil but she doesn't understand scrambles, & larks & hackcabs wh: give vague impressions of impropriety & curdle the blood in The Consort's veins.'[197]

Queen Victoria visited the Empress at Claridges on 11th December, when she recorded that she looked pretty, was in good spirits and talked a good deal about what she was seeing. During these few days Mérimée's old friend Sir Anthony Panizzi, the Librarian with whom she got on very well, showed Eugénie around the British Museum.

On 12th December Mr Claridge escorted his illustrious patron to the station. The Empress's visit to his establishment had been accidental, but word got around and set him on the road to success. That evening she sailed from Folkestone to Boulogne and was met inland at Amiens by the Emperor.

Two years later she told Lord Malmesbury of her delight with her 1860 journey.[198] She had either put the Leamington episode out of her thoughts, or come to terms with it.

She was not entirely free in her mind. In a letter to the Duchess of Manchester dated 21st January 1861, Lord Clarendon wrote that he had 'had 2 letters from her at Paris quite wild with one of her worst frights about the reports concerning herself', and mentions her forthcoming visit to Queen Victoria which was evidently worrying her: '[S]he will arrive in an agony of fear.' He then informs the Duchess that he had written to the Empress telling her to give no reason for having done what she liked, and not to excuse herself but to invite her kind friends to 'repair to a well known very warm place below.'[199] Not particularly useful advice, perhaps, but well intentioned.

Most of the record indicates, however, that the visit accomplished much of its intended purpose. The published letters of the English Madame Mohl, Lady Augusta Bruce's intimate friend, include a letter dated 12th November 1860, which states that 'the Empress is quite cured since she has been in England — she was tired of all the etiquette "he" imposed upon her and now feels as free as when she was a girl.'[200] (The date of Madame Mohl's letter, recorded as 12th November 1860, cannot be correct since the Empress did not even arrive in England until 14th November.)

Mme. Carette, an Imperial lady-in-waiting, wrote: 'After her visit to Scotland great changes took place in the tastes and habits of the Empress. The joyousness of her youth seemed to have vanished, to be superceded by those pleasing charms which belong to a woman matured by sorrow and revealed a sterner side to her nature.'[201]

Mérimée, equally observant, wrote of her in 1864 (when she was 38) remembering her as a child and young woman: 'Eugénie no longer exists, there is only an Empress I mourn and I admire.'[202]

CHAPTER TWELVE

Margaret: Eugénie

'In Spain mother-love is the holiest part of that deep love of the family which is one of the strongest and most fundamental traits in the Spanish temperament.'
  – Princess Pilar of Bavaria[203]

My reconstruction of the meeting of mother and daughter is as follows:

One dark November evening, Margaret and James received a message from a trusted member of the Empress's staff telling them of her forthcoming visit. They were carefully instructed as to what was expected of them. When the important day arrived the young couple were smuggled into the hotel through the tradesmen's entrance and swiftly taken upstairs to the Empress's suite. Eugénie had good reason to be nervous, yet how must it have been for Margaret? An empress would be alarming enough without the added stress of knowing she was her mother.

The reunion was tearful and emotional. Margaret's Lancashire accent sounded strange to the ear of a Spanish woman even though after her marriage she had continued to keep up her English studies.[204] Yet her daughter had a familiar petite frame and features.

A second meeting the following evening was easier than the first. The initial fearfulness on Margaret's part had diminished upon the realisation that an Empress was as much a flesh and blood woman as any other. Eugénie told her daughter of her love for Pepe who was Margaret's father, and her great distress at being forced to part with their baby daughter.

On their parting Eugénie gave James, Margaret's husband, a gift of money with instructions to remove his wife and child from Manchester to a healthier part of the country where she could secretly remain in touch with them. She promised that she would use her influence to ensure he found a good job. Knowing her own perilous position, she swore them to eternal secrecy.

On arriving in London and reflecting on this promise, she wrote to Alba, her brother-in-law, 'do you not think one requests too much of children.'[205]

CHAPTER THIRTEEN

Eugénie: Elsewhere

In 1863, in part at his Empress's urging and in part as an exercise of Imperial *la gloire*, Napoleon III propped the Austrian Archduke Maximilian up on the imperial throne of Mexico. In 1866, in the face of American opposition, he withdrew French troops from Mexico, setting in motion Maximilian's inevitable fall. The news of the tragic execution of the erstwhile Emperor Maximilian reached Paris on 19th June 1867. Eugénie was very distressed when she heard. Not only were her feelings touched, her reputation suffered. Her court opponents blamed her political dabbling for the debacle.

She decided to leave France for a while and visit her friend Queen Victoria, who was at her summer home, Osborne House on the Isle of Wight. Eugénie was not able to go at once because the arrangments were prolonged. On 11th July 1867 Mérimée wrote to his friend Sir Anthony Panizzi of the British Museum, who was known to both the Emperor and Empress. He had given the Empress a guided tour of the Museum on her 1860 visit, and had visited the imperial couple in turn at Biarritz in 1862. He also knew Madame de Montijo, to whom he sent regards through Mérimée at least once, on 16th August 1866.[206]

Mérimée's letter to Panizzi said: 'I am involved with the English affairs this had better be for you [only]. The Empress will spend four special days with the Queen. I think she will stay a day in London. She is incognito. It will be bad if you write this down. This is her life in your part of the world. This is confidential.'[207] On 19th July, he wrote to Panizzi again, saying that the Empress would be spending a few days *tête-à-tête* with the Queen and 'it seems improbable that she will go to England without spending a day in London.'[208]

According to *The Times*, accompanied by the Emperor, Eugénie left Paris in the early morning of 21st July for Le Havre to embark for England.[209] The Emperor was expected back in Paris that same evening. Yet a letter of Lord Clarendon's dated 21st July 1867 states, 'Eugénie arrived in England and went elsewhere from the coast'.[210]

The timescale is such that the imperial yacht *Reine Hortense* would not have left Le Havre before late evening on the 21st because it took eight hours to cross the Channel and it arrived at Portsmouth early the following morning, the 22nd. It anchored until afternoon near the Spit Buoy. *The Times* reported that on 22nd July 'a party of ladies and gentlemen from the yacht *including it was supposed the Empress*, landed at Southsea in the morning and spent some time on the Esplanade and Common and partook of luncheon at the Pier Hotel. Shortly after 2 pm the yacht weighed her anchor and the Empress arrived on a visit to H.M. The Queen shortly after 3 pm. No standard was hoist as the Empress travelled incognito'. [Emphasis added.]

The Times's reporter makes it clear that he was not certain that the Empress was with the party during the morning of the 22nd and Lord Clarendon refers in the past tense to her arrival on the 21st. Where had she been and why?

*Camden Palace in Chislehurst, and
Farnborough Hill, two of Eugénie's
residences during her exile in England*

Queen Victoria had written on 20th July to her daughter, but this letter had made no reference to the Empress or her coming visit. On 24th July 1867 she wrote 'The Dear Empress ... was very kind and amiable. She came quite incognito with only the Duchesse de Bassano and the Comte de Brissac and without attendants ... and by some extraordinary mischance – while we were all looking out, watching and waiting she arrived she came into the house!!! [HM's exclamation marks] You may imagine our horror from highest to lowest... – I sat with her for some little while we dined en famille. Yesterday morning [23rd July] I drove with her round the grounds and in the afternoon to the Swiss Cottage and Newport ... this morning before ten she embarked at our pier and steamed off to Brest.'[211]

To travel unnoticed was easy at a time when the wealthy could reserve both a cabin on the Channel boat and a compartment on the railway. The Emperor was evidently aware of his wife's plans and she had told Merimée in advance that she intended to go to London. Lord Clarendon seems to have known rather more in that she proposed going 'elsewhere'.

Queen Victoria and her entourage were looking out for her guest when they were taken by surprise; she arrived and went into the house unseen, presumably from an unexpected direction. If Empress Eugénie was aboard the imperial yacht when it sailed after lunch for the Isle of Wight, why was it not flying her standard? The evidence indicates that she had been on some jaunt of her own and arrived on the island at a different landing stage from that expected.

A letter to Panizzi from Mérimée shortly afterwards states, 'The tête-à-tête at Osborne was very intimate. I am told that S.M. ['Sa Majésté'] did not go to London.'

Again, Eugénie disappears through a hole in the his-

113

torical record. No mention of this affair is made in the two volumes of *The Life of Sir Anthony Panizzi KCB*, by Louis Fagan. Eugénie's published letters have a gap between 11th July 1866 and 8th October 1868. 1867 was the second time the court did not go to Compiègne in the autumn. The first such omission was 1860, the year of Paca's death and the Empress's journey to Scotland and Manchester.

Lord Clarendon wrote on a regular basis to the Duchess of Manchester. A selection of his letters dating between 1858 and 1869 have been published in *My Dear Duchess*. 1867 is the only year during this period for which no letter appears.[212] There are references to Maximilian in Mexico up to January 1866. The very next letter in this book is dated January 1868. Did he refer to the Empress and the execution of Maximilian in letters to the Duchess in 1867, and did she destroy them? According to the editorial matter in the volume, Clarendon was under the impression that she had destroyed every single one.

In the January 1868 letter Clarendon refers to the heir apparent Edward, Prince of Wales, visiting the Duchess of Manchester at Kimbolton manor house in Huntingdonshire, and says that 'he would like to know how it went off and whether he seems to have any generous feeling towards the "unfortunate" in Paris.' Eugénie? She would still be distressed and remorseful following her part in the chain of events which led to Maximilian's execution. Maximilian's widow Carlotta could not have been the 'unfortunate' referred to, as she was at that time with her brother in Belgium.

CHAPTER FOURTEEN

Margaret: American Cousins

In 1851, whilst Margaret was still living with the Pembertons, she is recorded as having been born at Atherton, Manchester (HO157 2287).

The census of 7th April 1861 (RG91921 p14) finds Margaret and her husband at Fordhouses, Coven Heath, near Bushbury in Staffordshire, both uniquely recorded as born in England. Evidently they did not know what to state as Margaret's birthplace and were playing safe. Subsequent census returns record her as having been born in Warrington, apart from 1881 which gives Manchester. James was described as an engine cleaner. As with other railways, most new hires at the LNWR worked first as a cleaner or other humble job.[213] Perhaps thanks to Eugénie's generosity in 1860, James promptly left his farm work for the London and North Western Railway, known as the 'Premier' or ' Royal' line because it transported Queen Victoria in the royal train.

That census[214] also records James's younger brother William as a lodger in Bushbury, a 19-year-old engine fireman (RG9 1931 54 p1). Unlike James he had not 'forgotten' that he was born at Astbury, Cheshire. William remained in Bushbury, working at various humble jobs on the railway, for the rest of his life.

Bushbury Junction is a few minutes' walk from Coven Heath. It was an important railway loop-line where the royal trains changed engines. The staff of the LNWR and Great Western Railways would take the opportunity to get together and chat, swapping stories and keeping up to date with the news.[215] The Bushbury Local History Society records that on 24th August 1861, whilst her train was at Bushbury being transferred to the LNW system on route from Gosport to Scotland, the Queen enquired as to who lived in a nearby house. Had she had a hand in James and Margaret's move?

For a young couple in clandestine contact with the outside world, the Bushbury sidings provided a highly convenient place for private meetings with passengers, and railway staff could always facilitate exchanges of gifts or letters. It is interesting to note that in 1881, 1891 and 1901 William Cartlidge's wife was a sub-postmistress and his daughter a rural letter carrier. This could have been useful for receiving and forwarding confidential mail.

By August 1862, when my husband's grandfather was born, James was described as a railway engine fitter. He and Margaret were still living at Coven Heath, which remains today in pleasant countryside, until 1874. Whilst living there they produced a further four children: Hannah Letitia, Howard Victor, Sara Jane Abigail and Maria Margaret Ellen.

By this point Queen Victoria quite likely knew that the Empress's illegitimate daughter and grandchildren lived close to Bushbury sidings. Eugénie may very well have turned to her close friend for assistance in securing James his new post on the 'Royal Line', or Victoria's efficient 'social intelligence' network (including agents like Lord Clarendon and her 'spy' Lady Augusta Bruce) may have worked out the truth. However it happened, the local people noticed that when the royal train stopped at Bushbury, the Queen would always come to the window and look out in the direction of Shaw Hall at Coven Heath.[216] Despite its grand-sounding name Shaw Hall was occupied by Thomas Ward, a farm labourer, Mary his wife, and their three children.[217] Queen Victoria's gaze would have been in the direction of the newly built railway Fordhouses where James and Margaret lived.

* * *

James Cartlidge had removed his family from the Manchester area just in time. In 1862, two years after the Empress Eugénie's visit, the American Civil War had triggered a 'cotton famine' in Lancashire. Without raw cotton from the American South, Manchester, the centre of the spinning and weaving trade, was in dire trouble. Donations of money poured in from many sources to help the workers, to be shared out among the unemployed. Large families received five to six shillings a week, but that was not enough to weather the crisis.[218] An Emigration Aid Society formed in April 1863, and by the last day of the month a thousand cotton workers left for New Zealand,[219] at that time undergoing intensive British settlement.

That same spring Margaret's foster-father Robert Pemberton made his own way to Philadelphia in the United States. Despite being fifty years old, on arrival he was drafted into the Union Army (in his case the Pennsylvania Volunteers) along with all other able-bodied men, to replace some of the many thousands slaughtered on the battlefields. By the autumn of 1863 Robert's wife Abigail and three children (Letitia Elizabeth, Sara Jane and Robert Landon) had joined him in America.[220]

The Poor Law Union Papers of Leigh make no reference to emigration assistance. The Emigration Entry Books and Land and Emigration Commission Papers — all searched on my behalf by a professional — have no relevant files. The Public Records Office lists 'Original Correspondence 1817-1896' under *America, British North Emigration Registers* at CO384 169. Perhaps there would be something about the Pembertons? But no, there is a gap between 1857 (No 99) and 1872 (No 100). The Emigration Register CO 327 2, for the period 1856-1863, holds very little and a single entry for 1863: not the Pembertons. A label on the front of the book states '*Letters regarding North American Emigration now (being 1863) entered in North America General Book*'. I could find no such book listed in the contents of the P.R.O.

How did Robert find the fare to America? How was his family supported? Could he get money back to England? What would have happened to them all had he been killed or maimed? Possibly the bounty given on his enlistment covered his family's fares.

The American Civil War ended in 1865, foredooming Napoleon and Eugénie's Mexican adventure as well. Robert and his family went to the town of Allegheny near Pittsburgh in 1865, and in 1870 moved to Wellsburg, West Virginia. The principal industries of the town were paper, glass, sheet metal cans and coal.

In 1873 when the children were twenty, eighteen and twelve, the Pembertons moved to New Martinsville in West Virginia, where they prospered. The Wetzel Genealogical Society and in particular Elizabeth Estlack Mullett have been very helpful and report along with other information that: 'It does appear that the Pembertons had money and social status'. Another clue to their status was a letter from Letitia Pemberton that turned up through Carol

118

Holland (the great-grand-daughter of Reuben Cartlidge, who was the youngest son of Margaret and James). Letitia's letter is dated 1931, by which time she was evidently an educated woman of means, a staunch churchgoer, and unmarried. Her letter which mentions her visit to England 30 years ago led to my tracing of the Pembertons' emigration and the discovery that in her early twenties Letitia had been buying properties and owned a millinery shop. When she left Lancashire aged 12 she would at best have had minimal schooling, and had worked from a very young age in a cotton mill. It was not until 1870 that there was even a very limited education for all of the children in the Lancashire mill towns.

The 1910 census of the Wetzel County, West Virginia, town of New Martinsville lists:

Letitia Pemberton, head of household, single, born England;
Abigail Potts, age 20, a trimmer in Letitia's shop;
Mary E. Cartlidge, age 9, great-niece, born Pennsylvania, father born England, mother Ireland.[221]

It seems probable that Mary was a daughter of Frederick Charles, a son of James and Margaret born in Rushall in 1874. Frederick Charles disappeared from the records in England, and is not mentioned in his father's will. Did he travel with his Aunt Letitia when she returned to America in 1901? Was he subsidised by his father at that particular time? The International Genealogical Index for the USA lists a Fred Cartlidge originating from Cheshire with no other information A Charles Frederick Cartlidge of Darby, Pennsylvania, born 26th April 1908, died 6th December 1988, may well have been his son and the younger brother of Mary. An index to the Philadelphia passenger lists 1800-1945 has recently appeared online. In it a Frederick Charles Cartlidge is listed, along with a Maria. Letitia Pemberton died on 23rd May 1935 and was buried in the family plot in the Williams Cemetery, next to her parents.

Sara Jane, daughter of Robert and Abigail, married William McGregory Hall in March 1877. Leonard, their son, was born in August 1877, and Sara died in 1939. Leonard and her grandson William both became attorneys and moved to Martin's Ferry, Ohio. There were two great-grandchildren, Susan Jane and William, Jr. With the help of the local newspaper, I made contact with Sara Hall's grandson Robert and his wife Mary Jo. Sara Hall died when Leonard S. Hall, Robert's father, was only eight years old. Robert's father re-married, and as so often happens in such circumstances, family history and mementoes were not handed down.

Robert Landon Pemberton, the son, became owner and editor of a newspaper, the *St Mary's Oracle*. He was also an author and a publisher. He died in 1944, his widow in 1954. Marjerie, the Pembertons' youngest daughter, never married.[222]

Maria Margaret Ellen Cartlidge, daughter of James and Margaret, appears in the 1901 census, listed as Margaret, housekeeper to widower Joseph Jenvey and his young sons. She is subsequently untraced but may have made her way to America. Carole Holland passed on to me copies of two letters one dated Jan 1853 and the other 30th August 1955, a copy envelope is addressed to Mrs Reuben Cartlidge (Clara) postmarked Mansfield Mass. USA. 'It is 55 years since I saw you,' she says and mentions their mother. It is signed 'your loving sister and old Johnr'. The later letter is signed 'from your aunt Emily',. Presumably her sister had died in the interim. The letters indicate that she was born in 1876 and had no children. I was told that her married name was Jenvey. It is probable that there was some connection with Maria Margaret Ellen Cartlidge, who was born in 1872.

120

CHAPTER FIFTEEN

Eugénie: The End of an Era

Lord Clarendon died on 27th June, in the eventful year of 1870. The pattern of Eugénie's correspondence follows the familiar formula: no letters written that year prior to November have been published so we cannot know her feelings on the death of Clarendon, a very old friend who may have been her natural father.

On 28th July Napoleon III and the 14-year-old Prince Imperial left Paris for the last time, on a military campaign against the Prussians. Eugénie again became Regent and left for the château of Saint-Cloud. On 6th August, a Saturday, as the Parisians anticipated news of a great victory and prepared to decorate the city in triumph, the Empress received a telegram from the Emperor: 'We are in full retreat.'

Two days after the humiliating French defeat at Sedan on 1st September 1870, the Empress received a further telegram from the Emperor, telling her that he had surrendered in order to save his army.

She returned to the Tuileries, which had been hurriedly taken over as a shelter for returning wounded soldiers. Her old friend Mérimée did what he could for her. Writing to their friend Panizzi in London, he said, 'I have seen the Empress. Her conduct is truly saintly and deserves admiration.'Eugénie spent the night of 3rd September destroying her private papers: tearing them into strips and soaking the fragments in hot water baths.[223] An angry mob collected outside, and her courtiers advised Eugénie to leave the city right away. She was smuggled through the Louvre and into a waiting cab through a side door, with nothing but what she stood up in. Her training in the mercurial Spanish court had taught her the value of preparedness, though: she had previously arranged the removal from the country of her personal jewellery.

Eugénie and her tiny entourage wandered around the city uncertain where to go, but eventually made for the house of Dr Evans, her dentist and good friend, who hid her overnight.

The next morning he escorted her to the coast, the Empress travelling under the guise of a sick woman in need of treatment. They reached Deauville at 11.30 p.m. and approached an Englishman, Sir John Burgoyne. His yacht *Gazelle* was moored nearby, and he agreed to take the Empress across the Channel. This proved to be a terrifying journey for her and a nerve-racking one for Sir John. Eugénie, as arranged, arrived on board at five past midnight on 7th September. Her arrival was a perilously near thing: two men had searched the vessel at 11.30 p.m.

At 6 a.m. Sir John cast off the vessel and took the pilot on board an hour later. The crossing was very rough. Sir John was impressed by the demeanor of the Empress, 'her charm, and her wonderfully good English', and said that the *Gazelle* behaved 'much better than we would have supposed she would have done'.[224] Upon arrival at the *Gazelle*'s home port of Ryde on the Isle of Wight, Sir John found that the Pier Hotel was full, and so he and the Empress, who was still accompanied by Madame le Breton and Dr. Evans, walked along to the New York Hotel.

All this is according to a letter written from Ryde by Sir John to 'My dear Robert' on 13th September, now owned by Peter Spencer, who has given me permission to reproduce it in this book. He is also the owner of the gold, diamond, and sapphire locket that the Tsar of Russia gave Eugénie as a wedding present. The Empress had fondled the locket during the voyage and later presented it to Sir John, asking him to pass it on to his descendants as a memento. Thus it came, through marriage, to its present owner.

At the Marine Hotel in Hastings, where the Empress stayed for a while, the young Prince Imperial was reunited with his mother.

The ever-faithful Prosper Mérimée had hurriedly left Paris for Cannes where he died on 23rd September 1870, just over a fortnight after his Empress's escape. 'All he had with him was a packet of stocks and shares and an enormous bundle of letters he was going to burn.'[225] These letters may have included those written to him by Madame de Montijo which have never been seen. But, still proud of the role he played in salvaging Eugénie's future thirty years before, he may have regretted their destruction. Around this time Mérimée had written to Maria, 'How I wish I could spend a few more hours with [Eugénie] and persuade her to write three hundred pages that will appear when God is willing and make future generations fall in love with her.'[226]

During the tumultuous following year his house in the Rue de Lille burned down, destroying his remaining books and papers. According to the unreliable Duque de

Ryde Sept 13th —

My dear Robert,

We were very much amused at your letter especially as it is my desire to deceive the telegraph clerks at Portsmouth I deceived you also — Any how was it not an odd thing that we should have been at Deauville & have been of much use to H. I. M. — On Tuesday at about noon I was on deck doing something or other, & two strangers came on board, & asked to see the yacht. I shewed them over, & one then bluntly told me he was commissioned by H. I. M. to ask me to take her on board under the protection of the British flag & take her to any port in England.

The first page of a letter from Sir John Burgoyne to 'My dear Robert', concerning the Empress's flight from France. The full text appears in Appendix 2 on pages 197-199

Alba, this fire was the reason the letters from Madame de Montijo were not available for publication.

Exactly thirty years after his death, Eugénie drove to Cannes with her husband's nephew Comte Primoli to visit the grave of her old friend.[227]

Shortly after arriving in England the exiled Empress found a house at Camden Place, near Chislehurst in Kent, where by a strange coincidence her husband had once been a guest of the previous owner, Henry Rowles. He had a Spanish wife and a daughter, Emily, who had been rumoured as a possible fiancée for the then-Prince Louis Napoleon.

The Emperor joined his wife and son in England in March 1871 following the cease-fire between France and Prussia. Their new home, Camden Place, a refurbished 16th-century building comprising twenty rooms plus kitchens and spacious grounds, was somewhat cramped with a household of 62 individuals. Queen Victoria referred to Camden as a small house with humble little rooms, especially in contrast to Windsor Castle and the vast palaces of France.

In September 1871 Eugénie sailed from Southampton to Lisbon on a three-month visit to her mother in Madrid. During her stay she was believed to have sold some of her Spanish property. Lord Cowley wrote to the Queen of Holland: 'I hear that the Empress has been enjoying herself in Spain far more than under the circumstances she ought to have done.'[228]

None of the letters Eugénie wrote that year have been published, so we cannot know to what he was referring. The Comtesse des Garets, a very young woman who had been in the Empress's service for only three years before the visit took place, recorded that the Spaniards' attitude towards the Empress astonished her. She was not, the Comtesse said, given the consideration and respect that she received in England, and 'it was obvious that as a young girl she had not been as popular as her sister'.[229] The Comtesse makes the assumption that her employer's unpopularity was due to her intelligence and independence as a girl. It was unlikely that the young Comtesse would have knowledge of scandals and gossip which occurred before her time, and even if she did know it would not have been politic to have recorded them in the Empress' lifetime.

In 1872 the Prince Imperial followed the family trade and enrolled as an artillery cadet at the Military College in Woolwich. During his time there he is reported to have had a lady friend, Charlotte Watkyns, and to have kept a small house in Jermyn Street, near to the college. The Prince found life difficult financially since his mother did not allow him sufficient for his needs, and according to a contemporary source, 'he could not take part in the entertainments or banquets at college for want of money.'[230] Another contemporary adds: 'General Fleury deplored the position almost of penury in which the Prince lived. He had to borrow money from Fleury when entertaining guests to lunch. He had to claim money from the Empress after the Emperor's death — owed for the purchase of horses, she was displeased. He tried to obtain a town house for the Prince Imperial in London — such as befitted his position — in vain'.[231] His biographer quotes the young Bonaparte: 'I never ask for anything, you see, in my position I can't allow myself to be refused.'[232]

At the end of June 1872 it was announced that the Emperor had sold his wife's jewels for £50,000. Clara Tschudi states that 'parsimony towards her son could only have been the desire to accumulate for his recall to France. She did however, indulge herself where her wardrobe and her library were concerned.'[233] During the last few weeks of the Prince's life he had owned money of his own.[234] Tschudi is mistaken in stating that the Empress had made his father's fortune over to him, however. Princess Baciocchi, daughter of the first Napoleon's sister Elisa, left him a substantial amount, but under the terms of the bequest he was not yet able to touch it.[235]

The health of the Emperor was not good but he made the best of things during his wife's absences, spending time at various resorts on the south coast of England until September when his health rapidly deteriorated.

The exiled Napoleon III died at Chislehurst on 9th January 1873, possibly from an overdose of chloral, following several operations for kidney stones.

Following the death of the Emperor, Eugénie indulged her love of travel and the company of young people. She entertained frequently, but did not become involved with the customary English country-house socialising. The only invitations she accepted, apart from a few private dinner parties, were from Queen Victoria. She was often the Queen's guest at Osborne Cottage on the Isle of Wight and at Abergeldie Castle near Balmoral at times when the Queen was in residence.

In the spring of 1876 Eugénie informed her lady-in-waiting the Comtesse des Garets that in August they would be going to Switzerland, where she had an inherited house at Arenenburg. From thence, their itinerary would take them to Italy for the winter, staying at a rented villa in Florence where the Prince Imperial would be joining them. In addition to des Garets, Eugénie's entourage for the trip included Comte and Comtesse Clary, Mme Le Breton, Dr Conneau and Comte Primoli. The Prince Imperial was in Arenenburg with two of his friends. The Comtesse, although she had kept a diary, said that she was unable to remember who they were.

After her son left at the beginning of October, the Empress divided her party into two. She sent the doctor and Comtesses Clary and Garets in one direction whilst she and the others went another. They were all instructed to meet in Florence at a specific hour and date. However, on 14th October the advance party was still in Milan when they should have been in Florence.

The Empress and her party arrived in Milan sooner than expected and she was annoyed to find the others still there. She sent them off to Florence immediately and they arrived the next day. Her own half of the party, once again with the Prince Imperial, arrived five days later on the 20th.[236] 'Not a few there [in Florence] recalled Eugénie in her unmarried days when she had been fast, wild and mysterious'.[237]

The party remained in Florence until early April. At that point, they set off for Spain, travelling via Rome, Naples, Sorrento, Capri, Syracuse, Malta, Gibraltar and thence to the Spanish port Malaga and overland to Seville. Here Queen Isabella and the Infanta received them, being in residence in the newly refurbished (reportedly in abominable taste) Alcazar.

From Seville the Empress went to Cordova, and at the suggestion of the Governor took her reluctant party on an uncomfortable trip by railway and mule coach to see the then almost unknown gorge of Ronda. Their lodgings were grim and none too clean but nevertheless they stayed for a week. Perhaps the stark scenery or the experience of living hard inspired a reminiscent Eugénie to tell Comte Primoli a redacted version of her 1840 adventure.

The next stage of the journey was by train via Toledo to Madrid, where the Empress was due to visit her mother. Whilst in Madrid and organising her return journey to England, Eugénie received a letter from her son. He complained that he had already been 'an orphan' for two months and made known his disapproval of her intention to return via France: 'I will never place my foot in France save as a leader ... I could not bear to mingle with people who would remain indifferent'.[238]

The party was back in England in good time for the 'season' at Cowes on the Isle of Wight.

Around this time the name of the Prince Imperial became romantically linked with Queen Victoria's youngest child, Princess Beatrice. Whether or not the young couple were actually attracted, much less involved, can only be speculation but according to Lady Lytton, Queen Victoria's lady-in-waiting, the Empress was very much in favour of a relationship. Queen Victoria, on the other hand, did not want any liasion for Beatrice, who was expected to stay at home as her companion. After the Prince's death, the Princess announced her engagement to Prince Henry of Battenburg (whom she married). The Queen did not speak to her for six months. When Princess Beatrice died a framed photograph of the Prince Imperial was found in her bedroom.

He seems to have been a popular young man. When he celebrated his coming of age in England, his French guests were very impressed by the speech he made.[239] After leaving Woolwich, the Prince, who had been brought up to believe that glory on the battlefield was a highly desirable achievement, went out to Zululand with the permission of Queen Victoria. Princess Beatrice's biographer speculates: 'Could it have been that she wanted him out of the way?'[240]

It was there that the Prince Imperial was killed in a skirmish with Zulu warriors on 1st June 1879. While he and Lieutenant Jahleel Carey, who had been assigned to look after him, were dismounted, the Zulus ambushed their party. Whilst hurriedly remounting to escape, the girth holding the Prince's saddle in place broke, and he fell to the ground. The Zulus closed in. According to the surgeon's evidence, the Prince Imperial died from eighteen *assegai* wounds to the front of his body, demonstrating that he had boldly faced up to his killers.

It has been said with justification that had he been able to afford better tackle for his mount, this would never have happened. The *Century Magazine* of June 1893 reported that the girth was a band of paper-faced 'leather', though quite what this implies is not clear.[241] General Fleury had wanted the Prince to buy his tackle and saddlery from the best maker in England but the Empress thought that the 'Stores' would be cheaper and this was from where she bought his entire outfit.[242]

These comments were very cruel but cannot be dismissed, since Eugénie had a reputation for meanness despite Princess Marie Louise's characterization of her 'great and generous nature'.[243] Other judgements are harsher: 'All her life Eugénie had a tendency to meanness with the funds, except in the matter of arraying her person or increasing her library.'[244] The Empress had 'a want of generosity … she had not the princely art of giving even trifling marks of remembrance on appropriate occasions … though for her own concerns she is shrewd and cunning'.[245] Clara Tschudi's claim that Eugénie was saving for her son's return to France is more charitable.[246]

The bad news reached England on the 14th June. Queen Victoria was told before the Empress. Lord Sydney was given the difficult task.[247] The Queen wrote to Vicky, her eldest daughter, on 21st June, 'Poor poor Empress – who has lost her all, her only child'. On 25th June the Queen wrote again, 'I send you here an account of the heart-rending visit [to the Empress] which you can show Fritz but no one else, because it would be a breach of confidence to repeat all she said to me.'[248]

Had Eugénie, at this time of great emotion, spoken to the Queen of her other child?

She then spent three months on her own, apart from her companion the Comtesse des Garets, at Abergeldie Castle at the invitation of the Queen who, accompanied by John Brown and Princess Beatrice, visited her regularly.

E.E.P. Tisdall states that the Prince's old lover 'Charlotte Watkyns, eight years after the Prince Imperial's death appeared with a clutter of princely love letters and an Imperial bastard.'[249] Eugénie is reported to have said that the 'infant' [sic] had been too long in the womb to be her son's child, implying that Tisdall made a mistake, and meant eight weeks, or even months, after the Prince's death. By eight months a few weeks, or by eight years a few months, one way or the other would be undetectable. Alternatively the Empress was emphatically, yet illogically denying that her son could have fathered a child.

Referring to this period, the Comtesse des Garets writes, 'As for the idea of leaving England, it never occurred to her, her natural home was there because her dead were there.'[250]

Would it be her dead or her living relatives who would keep her in England? Eugénie did have the bodies of her husband and son moved when she moved house to Farnborough.

The following year Eugénie paid a sad visit to Africa, accompanied by an entourage of seven. She travelled eight hundred miles in a four-horse carriage to the place where her son had fought and been killed, spending the anniversary night at the foot of his memorial cross, which had been erected on instructions from Queen Victoria.

CHAPTER SIXTEEN

Margaret: Eugénie Again

'Eugénie earned the privilege of veiling her life in the privacy which is generally denied to historical personages.'
– *Philip W. Sergeant, The Last Empress of the French (1907)*[251]

By 1871 the deposed Empress of the French was living in a modest English country house, Camden Place, at Chislehurst. In her biography *The Tragic Empress*, the Comtesse des Garets reproduced a letter from her mistress dated 6th August 1871. It had been written to her when the Comtesse was away in France visiting her parents. This letter mainly concerns a request for Marie, as the Empress called her, to bring home certain flowers and bushes from the Tuileries garden. The Comtesse tells that she then received another letter requesting that she cut short her holiday in order to go to Spain with her mistress in early September.

On 9th September of that year Empress Eugénie left for a visit to her mother and her two nieces, the daughters of her late sister who had in happier days lived with her in Paris. Travelling to Southampton by train and accompanied by Marie, she boarded the *Oneido* and sailed the same night for Lisbon. The Duque de Alba met the ladies in Portugal and escorted them on the long slow train journey to Madrid and thence to Quinta de Miranda, Eugénie's old home at Carabanchel just outside the city.[252] The Comtesse stayed only a few days at the none-too-comfortable house before moving to the grander and livelier Liria Palace in Madrid at the invitation of the understanding Duque de Alba. Eugénie remained with her mother until November by which time the Condesa de Montijo and the former governess Miss Flower had moved into their winter home, the Casa Ariza on the Plaza del Angel in Madrid. Eugénie and Marie returned to England in November.

Margaret's fifth baby, Sara Jane Abigail (Abbie), had been born in July 1869 and Margaret did not become pregnant again until July 1871. Did she secretly meet her mother in September of that year at Southampton, and accompany her to Spain? It would have been a perfect opportunity for Margaret to see her native country and for mother, daughter, and grandmother to get to know one another. In April 1872 Margaret gave birth to her third daughter, christened as Maria[253] (the name of the Comtesse de Montijo) Margaret (the name of her mother) Ellen (the name of Betsy Pemberton's mother).

* * *

The Comtesse de Garets, in referring to her 'few brief notes' which were her sources for her book, wrote: 'I possess another very precious source of reference, the letters which the Empress used to write me each year during the month's holiday which I spent in France with my family. I possess a hundred of them.' She goes on to say that most of their content is insignificant, and that 'their more intimate passages must always remain a sealed book even if I were tempted to disclose the vital affection and maternal solicitude to which they bear witness'.[254]

If this affection and maternal solicitude of the Empress was directed towards the Prince Imperial or even to Marie herself, it was to the Empress's credit and there is no valid reason why she should want to hide it. This leads to the supposition that there were references to Margaret.

CHAPTER SEVENTEEN

Eugénie: Her Only Love

Pepe de Alcañices had not remained idle. His social circles continued to overlap with Eugénie's and, as we have seen, his affairs with Queen Isabella II of Spain and with Madame Morny (who he eventually married) likely stung the Empress even more personally than they did politically. However, his dalliance with Isabella changed Spanish politics significantly, since Pepe (a descendant of Alfonso XI) sired the Prince of Asturias, the boy who would become King Alfonso XII of Spain.

Pepe was not Queen Isabella's only lover. According to report, all her children had different fathers. In 1864, for example, a palace guard fathered her daughter Eulalia, a fact that Alfonso XIII related 'with some glee' to Queen Victoria's grand-daughter Princess Alice.[255] Other candidates have been proposed as Alfonso XII's natural father, although again the evidence for Pepe is strong. Not only do we have the characteristic hole in Eugénie's correspondence around that time, we have a letter from another observer.

In August 1869, Prosper Mérimée — who of course knew Pepe well as a youth from his attendance on the de Montijos — wrote to Jenny Dacquin, 'the prince of Asturias

135

Napoleon III and Eugénie in England. But who was her true love?

is very "gentil" with an intelligent air. He resembles * * * and children of the time of Vélasquez.'[256] ('Vélasquez' refers to the 17th-century Spanish painter.) Did the writer or the editor insert those asterisks? It hardly matters; had the Prince resembled his mother there would have been no need to obliterate the name, leading to the assumption that Mérimée names the likely father in his letter.

By that time, Isabella was living in Paris, as her own armed forces had overthrown her in 1868. On 10th October, a disapproving Queen Victoria wrote: 'The Queen of Spain is a most unfortunate woman. Every excuse must be made for her private conduct — on account of her cruel marriage [to the homosexual Francisco de Asis]. But her misgovernment is to me incredible.'[257] Nevertheless, out of *noblesse oblige* if nothing else, Victoria invited Isabella to stay at Balmoral Castle in 1890.

Pepe, meanwhile, was looking out for his royal son's interests. 'It was Pepe who suggested to Queen Isabella that she abdicate in favour of her son,'[258] reports the historian Petrie, and other sources concur: '... on June 25th, the Emperor and Sexto [Pepe] at last persuaded Isabella to abdicate irrevocably to clear the path for Alfonso'.[259] Princess Pilar writes, 'He dedicated all his time and energy and spent his large private fortune in helping to bring about the restoration of the Spanish monarchy in the person of Afonso XII.'[260]

Alfonso succeeded to the throne of Spain at the end of 1874. Pepe de Alcañices, now the Duque de Sexto, held the post of *'grand maître'* of the Palace during his reign.[261] Like father, like son: King Alfonso's second wife, Maria Cristina was annoyed and upset by her husband's constant infidelity. On one occasion she boxed Pepe's ears for introducing him to a dancer with dubious morals.[262]

Eugénie would have had a strong affinity towards the king as the reputed son of Pepe. On 8th October 1874 the

Empress, 48 years old, wrote to her niece Louisa, telling her that Pepe had visited her at Camden Place whilst escorting Alfonso on his way to Sandhurst Military College.[263] Princess Pilar observed that this, their first meeting since Eugénie had become a widow, 'must have been very moving since he was the only man she ever loved – but he loved her sister.'[264] She had never shown an interest in any other man.

The Comtesse des Garets, referring to her visit to Spain with Eugénie in 1877, writes 'I cannot remember whether it was at Aranjuez or Granja that King Alfonso XII visited her. The Empress was very fond of that charming prince, and he always remembered with gratitude the country [France] which has sheltered him in exile.'[265] Aranjuez and La Granja are the royal summer palaces, both near Madrid.

Princess Pilar states that 'the Marquess de Alcañices [Pepe] was entirely and disinterestedly devoted to the Spanish Royal Family'. She tells that Eugénie and Queen Isabella remained firm friends throughout their lives, and says more plausibly that there was reason to suppose the Empress used her considerable influence with Queen Victoria in favour of Isabella's son.[266]

King Alfonso XII's much-loved first wife Mercedes died suddenly and mysteriously in 1878, shortly after she was married. Still only in her teens, she had supposedly suffered a chill. Pepe had encouraged the match although Queen Isabella disapproved strongly (and did not attend the ceremony) because Mercedes was her sister's child. Mercedes' father, the Duc de Montpensier, had plans to displace Alfonso and to personally succeed his sister-in-law Isabella on the throne.

King Alfonso's second wife, Maria Cristina of Austria, bore him two daughters, Mercedes and Maria Teresa, before he died quite suddenly. Not yet thirty, he succumbed to 'consumption' in November 1885. Montpensier's plot, if plot there was, was thwarted six months later, when Maria Cristina produced a son, born King Alfonso XIII.

After Alfonso XII's death, Eugénie wrote to her nephew Carlos, 16th Duque de Alba, on 26th November 1885 saying, 'the Marquis d'Alcañices will be plunged into anguish since he loved him [Alfonso] as his own son'.[267] She told Carlos, 'I have telegraphed him,' and on 27th December she wrote again that she 'would like to know if Alcañices has received my letter'.

Pepe de Alcañices was a guest of the Imperial couple on at least one occasion during the reign of the Second Empire. There are eighteen references to Pepe in Eugénie's published letters. Extracts from her *Lettres Familières* show that throughout his lifetime he was in her thoughts. On 9th April 1857 she wrote to Paca, 'I pray you give me a little word of Pepe.' On 1st January 1875, when she was almost fifty, she wrote to her niece Louisa, to 'please give the attached letter to Marquise de Alcanise'.

On 29th January she complains that 'I have had no reply from Pepe.' Then on 8th March, 'I am profoundly wounded that the Duke of Sexto has not replied to my *two* letters.' [Emphasis added.] On 18th June at the age of 64, she wrote to her niece Rosario, saying, 'Alcañices intends to come. I hope that you will too'.

Writing from her villa Cynros at Cap Martin in the south of France on 24th April 1896, just before her seventieth birthday, she was evidently thinking about the place where she had spent the first night of her July adventure in 1840: '[A]nd what happiness it would be for me at this moment to see everyone again and go to Romanillos'. On 22nd October 1897 she wrote that she had telegraphed Pepe to tell him of the death of Comte Niebla, but she did not have his address and so had just put 'Palais' Madrid.

In June 1898 a 72-year-old Eugénie wrote the letter to Rosario from Paris in which she makes the very last mention of Pepe in her published papers. She wrote that she had seen Pepe de Alcañices 'of whom I spoke when in Spain'. It seemed that he was hoping to protect the Spanish royal family 'until the day of deceptions'.[268]

Her final meeting with her beloved was, according to her great-nephew the 17th Duke of Alba, at his home the Liria Palace in Madrid in 1904. The couple, both long since widowed, were discussing old times. Eugénie tasked her friend, saying, 'You never would marry me.' Pepe retorted, 'No, not even today would I want to marry you.'[269] The almost 80-year-old Eugénie is reported to have roared with laughter. She had acted in plays as a girl when at home at Carabanchel and later at Compiègne after her marriage. Was she still acting then or did she no longer care?

Alfonso XIII, the probable grandson of Pepe, married Victoria Eugenia of Battenburg, known as 'Princess Ena', the grand-daughter of Queen Victoria and god-daughter of Empress Eugénie, on 31st May 1906. The bride was received into the Catholic faith in the Empress's private chapel at her home in Farnborough, where after the ceremony the newlyweds spent part of their honeymoon. The best bedroom had been decorated in sky-blue damask in their honour. Pepe was still alive at the time, but there is no record as to whether he was present at the ceremony. The marriage of Alfonso to the daughter of Princess Beatrice, the girl Eugénie would have chosen as her son's wife, probably gave the Empress some satisfaction.

The day Pepe died, 30th December 1909, he ordered his confidential secretary to burn, in his presence, all the letters he had received from three correspondents: his wife Sophie, Paca de Montijo, and Eugénie.

CHAPTER EIGHTEEN

Letitia

When my husband and I were told of the Pemberton descent from the Empress I vividly recall that Uncle Bob Cartlidge said that 'the Pembertons' — plural — were her descendants. This made no sense at the time but with greater knowledge I can pose the question: Was Letitia Elizabeth Pemberton a second illegitimate daughter of Eugénie de Montijo? In her letter to Reuben Cartlidge dated 15th December 1931 Letitia refers to her visit to England 30 years earlier. Empress Eugénie had died in 1920.

In 1850, the year of Letitia's conception, Eugénie was at home in Madrid. According to her family letters — there are only two published for that year — she was in Seville in May and Wiesbaden on 22nd July. There is no clue to her whereabouts in June. Her beloved Pepe did not take up with Queen Isabella II until 1856, and did not marry Sophie until 1868. Perhaps as important, her rival for his affections, Paca, was happily married by then. Eugénie may well have been seeing Pepe in early 1850, perhaps even with the foolish intention of becoming pregnant again since she was always desperately in love with him and hoping to oblige him to marry her.

The letters of Prosper Mérimée to Madame de Montijo in 1850 and 1851 contain more cryptic and ambiguous remarks, not typical of the correspondence, yet not as emotional in tone as those of the troubled time ten years earlier. In August of 1850 he is telling his old friend that he had been hoping that Eugénie would have 'told him all that he had asked of her'. A reference to 'Madame X' appears again. Is this the same Madame X, the potential wet nurse of 1840? A letter dated November 1850 ends 'goodbye dear Comtesse, carry yourself well [meaning 'keep your chin up'] and come to see us'. It ends with the resigned-sounding sentiment 'We try to be wise' and with '*expressiones*' — a rather more formal greeting than usual — 'to the girls'.[270]

A letter from Paris dated 12th January 1851 refers to medical matters, including the use of chloroform. This letter ends with '*expressiones*' to D. Lucas (the major domo who had his own ambiguous part in the 1841 adventure) and notes that 'It is in March I think that we shall see'.[271]

If Eugénie was having another child, the Pembertons would have been the obvious choice for foster parents. They were already party to de Montijo secrets and had proved reliable. If Letitia was a child of Eugénie, she must have been born earlier than the date given on her birth certificate, 5th May (Eugénie's birthday — a coincidence?) 1851. Abigail registered this birth on 3rd June, and signed with a cross. The family address given was 18 Trumpet Street, Manchester. By 1855 the Manchester Directory lists the Pembertons at 9 Omega Place, Jordan Street, Manchester.

Eugénie was in Madrid in early March according to the newspapers *La Epoca* and *El Heraldo*.[272] Mérimée expected something to happen in March. Mother and daughter had travelled to England by April 1851 (the date is unrecorded)[273] ostensibly to visit the Great Exhibition in May. They were in Paris by 10th May and in London again by 21st June. This was the period when her mother was desperately trying to marry Eugénie off – but she was not interested.

* * *

The social standing and financial position of the Pembertons in West Virginia was notable considering their humble origins, and may have been assisted through subsidisation from the Empress. Were they included in the annuities – 'those which I suppress' – referred to in only one of the two otherwise identical copies of her will?

At the time of his death, Robert had not worked for many years. His obituary in 1897 describes him as 'an old citizen of Maple Avenue. An upright and honest man and highly respected.'[274]

The Mary Cartlidge who was living with Letitia in West Virginia in 1910 was almost certainly a grand-daughter of James and Margaret. Any descendants and those of her siblings could be numerous since she had an Irish, possibly Catholic mother. Do they have any knowledge of Margaret Cartlidge's interesting history? They could well know more than the English descendants since the distance from Europe was at the time formidable.

My husband Derek, as a child in Egypt in the 1930s where his father was serving in the Royal Engineers, remembers news arriving of the death of a relative of some evident importance.

Letitia Pemberton died on 21st May 1935. About this time Robert Cartlidge Jr (born 1891) went on a mysterious family mission subsequently located as West Virginia. Perhaps he wished to discover whether his father, as her nephew, was one of Aunt Letitia's heirs. Whatever his mission his hopes came to nothing. He told his wife on his return on that he had been 'blocked'. We had heard from my mother-in-law a vague story of an 'old man who

143

would not part with the papers' because, she believed, of a scandal. We assumed she referred to her father-in-law James Robert Samuel Cartlidge, whose elder son we now know had visited Robert L. Pemberton Jr, who was the owner and editor of a newspaper.

My husband remembered his father corresponding with a newspaper editor uncle in the USA whom we assumed to be a Cartlidge.

We now know that the newspaper was the *St Mary's Oracle* and that the editor uncle was Robert Pemberton, who had invited his 'great-nephew' Robert to emigrate and join him. Jean Cartlidge, when in her nineties, remarked that they had often wondered 'where they would have been had they gone'. She told me that prior to his visit her husband had employed a professional genealogist but she could not − or would not − say why.

After he returned home, his wife told us, Robert said very little, and destroyed the papers.

* * *

In February 2002 we had a surprise visit from Dennis, the son of one of Reuben Cartlidge's daughters.. Reuben had undertaken the job of executor to his father (his elder brothers had renounced probate). After his death Dennis's mother and aunts cleared the family papers and photographs which he described as being in a long horizontal frame. He has no knowlege of their fate.

CHAPTER NINETEEN

Eugénie: Sisters

'It would be an impertinence to attempt to disturb her privacy. What is to be made public about her existence at Farnborough can only be revealed, if ever, by her own permission.'
— *Philip W. Sergeant, The Last Empress of the French (1907)*[275]

A close friendship had developed between the Queen and the Empress, who now addressed each other as *'ma chere soeur'*. They were from totally different cultural and social backgrounds and their early years could not have been more different. Now they were social equals, although Queen Victoria could never quite decide whether an Empress was a higher rank than a Queen. This would seem to be the reason she was so pleased to become 'Empress of India'.

The two great ladies shared many memories and enjoyed recalling earlier and happier days when their husbands were alive and the two couples had exchanged visits. Birth and death were frequent occurences in the Victorian age and mourning was an expected and acceptable part of life. A reluctant mother of nine children, Queen Victoria was far from happy about her rapidly breeding

Empress Eugénie in later life

family. In July 1868 she wrote to her eldest daughter, the Crown Princess of Prussia, that they reminded her of the rabbits in Windsor Great Park.

They had ample opportunity to discuss intimate family matters during their strolls together in the Scottish hills. Their intimacy would be theraputic for both. Who knows what confidences the two empresses exchanged?

When Queen Victoria's ghillie and reputed lover John Brown died, Eugénie was one of the very few people to send flowers to his funeral. Lady (Linthorn) Simmons, wife of the governor of Woolwich Military Academy, wrote in her diary a week after Brown had died that her friend the Empress was both compassionate and entertaining about the Queen's loss. She believed that since he was a servant and not a gentleman this should prevent any slander. Lady Simmons continued that, 'she added more I was not to repeat,' and the governor's wife kept her word.[276]

In 1879 Maria de Montijo died, and in order to attend to her affairs Eugénie returned home to Madrid. There her parents Conde and Condesa de Montijo lie buried in a modest mausoleum in San Lorenzo Cemetery. In May 1886 the sad news had arrived that the de Montijos' old home at Carabanchel near Madrid had been badly damaged by a tornado and, as if that were not enough, phylloxera had ravaged her vineyards.

In March 1881 Eugénie moved out of Camden Place and lived for a short time at Coombe Cottage, near Kingston-on-Thames, which she rented from the Baring family (Baring Bros Archives are with Guildhall and available for consultation only with owner's permission), before moving to Farnborough Hill in Hampshire. She had this house altered and a church, St Michael's Abbey, built in the grounds, as well as a mausoleum for the re-internment of the bodies of the Emperor and their son.

On 3rd June 1886 Eugénie 'entertained a simple, genuine couple, a Mr and Mrs Ayliff from the Cape of Good Hope, who had entertained the Empress when she visited Zululand to see the place where her son had died.' Another guest that day was 'a young Captain Pemberton of the Royal Engineers'.[277] (He was Ernest St-Clair Pemberton, son of Charles Pemberton of Cleveland Terrace, London. The Captain had been at Woolwich Military Academy at the same time as The Prince Imperial. The name is a coincidence, as he has no connection with the other Pembertons in this book.)

Agnes Carey writes also about a particular visitor of the Empress at Farnborough, identifying her merely by the initial 'H'. This lady arrived at the house at 11 a.m. on 9th October 1886. 'H arrived, we showed her the State carriages before lunch and afterwards went for a drive all through Aldershot both North and South Camps. She left at 7.27 (the 7.27 train arrived Waterloo at 8.40pm) having very much enjoyed her day and the Empress's kindness. I am sorry that H did not see the embroidery; it is like a lovely painting of flowers and will certainly go down to posterity with honour.'[278] Who could this mysterious lady be and why the secrecy? Carey names everyone else in her book.

The French government eventually gave their former Empress permission to visit France. This was good news since, not surprisingly, she did not care for the English winters. The Bonapartists had become increasingly irrelevant, consumed with in-fighting. Prince Napoleon Joseph Charles ('Plon-Plon'), the son of Napoleon I's brother Jerome, had disinherited his own eldest son Napoleon Victor, who the Prince Imperial had designated his own successor in his will. Upon his death in 1891 the Bonaparte family visited Eugénie, who was wintering in San Remo. The press became interested in their two days of discussions but was told they only concerned family matters.[279]

During 1894-1895, Eugénie built Villa Cyrnos at Cap Martin near Menton in the south of France, where she had acquired a tongue of land projecting into the sea. Careful design gave sea views from every room. Later she built a similar house, Villa Teba, in the grounds for her guests. The architecture is reminiscent of Gunnersby Park in West London, once owned by Princess Amelia, daughter of King George II, and subsequently by the Rothschild family who were Eugénie's friends.

Queen Victoria visited her 'dear sister' at Cap Martin in the spring of 1898 when she was staying nearby at Cimiez, close to Nice.[280] She later made a second visit with her daughter Vicky, the 'Empress Frederick' of Germany.

Travelling to Scotland with the Queen became an annual event for Eugénie, until August 1898 when she declined the usual invitation because she found their destination too cold.[281] But before that date, Eugénie and Victoria often rode the 'Royal Line', the LNWR, north to Balmoral. On such royal runs seats were carefully allocated to all the Queen's guests, and 'the detailed instructions about the journey caused considerable amusement'.[282]

Some of the detailed instructions caused comment as well: 'Her [Queen Victoria's] Royal progresses became the subject of considerable public interest, and it was noted that her train sometimes made a lengthy stop at Leamington. Strange rumours ran around as to the reason for this, one being that in the early hours she had a rendezvous there with an illegitimate royal relation – the identity whom was kept secret'.[283] Given the frequent presence of Eugénie on the train, and the presence of her 'illegitimate royal relation' near Leamington, this rumour is highly suggestive.

Study of Victoria's letters to her eldest daughter shows her to have been a just and kindly woman who saw the best in everyone. It can reasonably be assumed that Her Majesty knew Eugénie's secret, perhaps long before the Empress confided in her. A compassionate woman with a strong sense of family, it is in character for her to arrange that 'her dear sister' could meet her daughter late at night in the comfort and privacy of the royal train.

Residents of Leamington remembered Eugénie visiting the Spa. A centenarian lady told journalist Charles Lines, who passed the information on to me in 1989, that as a child she was very worried on hearing that the French Empress was to visit since she expected her to be bringing an army! Leamington was sufficiently far off the beaten track to be convenient for private reunions. The townspeople believed that the Empress wished to see the places her husband had visited when he had lived there in the 1830s.

Despite the fact that she would say, 'I died in 1870,' Eugénie continued to lead a very full life. Perhaps her secret daughter — the 'succour' referred to by her old friend Mérimée and about whom only a few other souls would have known — played a part.

She never let it be forgotten that she had been Empress of France, and presided over a miniature court at Farnborough where she was always referred to as '*Sa Majesté*'. At the end of each day she bade good night to her guests by performing her renowned Andalusian curtsey.

In addition to entertaining at home she went out frequently but selectively, accepting invitations to dine with a few very close friends. The only house parties she would attend were those held by the Queen. In addition she made good use of her yacht, *Thistle*, which she had bought from the Duke of Hamilton, sailing as far afield as Constantinople in 1910. In Queen Victoria's time there were several artificial ice rinks in London patronised by the upper classes.[284] Eugénie had learned to skate along with the Emperor on the frozen waters of the Bois de Boulogne in Paris and she continued in England, probably at the Prince's Skating Club in Knightsbridge.

Queen Victoria died in January 1901. There are two letters of Eugénie's published for that month; her address is not given and she does not mention the queen's death. She was probably at Cap Martin, where in April she entertained the queen's youngest child Princess Beatrice, who celebrated her 44th birthday during the visit.

When travelling to and from her French home the former Empress would break her journey in Paris, where she stayed at the Hotel Continental, overlooking the Tuileries Gardens and the site of the Palace, her old home. She would wander alone in the gardens, sadly recalling the past. At least once she went to nearby Compiègne where the Palace in the forest remains intact. Whilst touring the rooms she gave way to tears on finding the notch on a door which had been cut to mark the height of her young son.

In England on an undated occasion she is recorded to have paid a spontaneous visit to Broadmoor Asylum whilst out driving. Broadmoor is today a prison hospital for mentally afflicted offenders, situated in the middle of Dartmoor in Devon and a very long way from her home.[285] There is also reference to a visit to an unspecified county asylum where the inmates played in her honour the Second Empire anthem *Partant pour la Syrie*.[286] Surely there was prior notice of her visit, since the former French national anthem would seem unlikely to have been part of their repertoire.

It was usual for these institutions to have an orchestra. At Burntwood Asylum in Staffordshire where Margaret's second son J. Robert S. Cartlidge [in later life

151

he used only Robert] was head attendant, the primary qualification for such staff members was to be a musician. Robert was a flautist.

CHAPTER TWENTY

Margaret: Margaret's Family

'It is acknowledged by the Public Records Office that matters which are close to the royal family, or concern intelligence operations, are closed to the public.'
– Michael Occleshaw, The Romanov Conspiracies[287]

Around 1876 Margaret and James and their six children moved to Rushall, near Walsall, presumably to a larger house. Here four more sons were born, Jesse William in 1877, Reuben (later to be known as Carroty because of his red hair) in 1878, and Sydney Doctor in July 1880. James Pemberton the brother of Robert and his wife Dinah had previously given this strange name to their son in May 1860. Sydney died in April 1881 at 59 Cecil Street in Rushall. His mother, by then forty years old, continued her busy life with five unmarried sons and three daughters living at home. By 1891 her family, now at 81 Mill Street, was reduced to Reuben aged ten and Jesse aged eleven.

Around that time, one Alice White (born 1880) saw 'Princess' Eugénie – the title would be easily confused by a child – at Snow Hill Station, Wolverhampton. Alice lived on nearby Pearson Street, and was the grandmother of Mrs Diana Bevan of Newcastle, Staffordshire. who wrote to me 'I had always wondered what she [Eugénie] was doing there'. The Coach and Horses, a hotel at No 59 Snow Hill, advertised in the local directory proudly stating that it leased out high-quality coaches and horses with drivers. Wolverhampton is about five miles from Rushall where Margaret was living and equidistant from her earlier home at Coven Heath. Both Rushall and Coven Heath lay just a few stops along the LNW Railway. At this period James Cartlidge worked as an engine driver and would spend several days at a time away from home. It is a reasonable assumption that the Empress's private visit to the district was to meet her daughter, possibly by discreetly sending a carriage to collect her. It does not seem likely that, being as recognisable as she evidently was, she would have risked visiting Margaret at her home.

The Wolverhampton Archives Office has no record of any visit by Empress Eugénie, although they have records of royal visits in addition to their local newpaper archives. There is nothing published elsewhere to indicate any visit of the Empress to Wolverhampton.

However, the records are far from comprehensive in any case. For example, current Dorset residents speak of the Empress's visits to Bournemouth, where she stayed at the Royal Bath Hotel. The Hampshire Records Office has no knowledge of such visits. Rosamund Lodge has written to tell me of visits to Brighton, where Eugénie stayed at the boarding house of her great-grandmother, Anna Kirchner (*née* Bardon), a Frenchwoman. Nothing has been published or appears in the Empress's published letters regarding any visits to Bournemouth, although

*James and Margaret Cartlidge, perhaps on
the occasion of their golden wedding in 1910*

Napoleon III was at Bognor and Brighton in August 1872 and was joined later by the Prince Imperial travelling from Scotland.[288]

James Cartlidge's career with the LNWR is puzzling, as it did not follow the structured pattern of a railway worker. Information from some of the birth certificates and all of the relevant census returns tells that after his first post as a cleaner in 1861 he became an engine fitter in 1862, at the age of 25.

He held eleven different posts on the railway before being recorded as a railway engine driver in 1881 to 1896. followed by a further three posts before retiring.

His daughter-in-law Jean, widow of Robert, said that he became a line foreman for the Carlisle to Crewe section. In October 1910 at the time his wife died in Rushall he is described as railway servant (retired). In an interview given to a local newspaper in 1927 James confirms that he worked for the railway for nearly fifty years, retiring 'some 20 years ago'.

A document concerning an LNWR Provident pension and dated 1911 is in the hands of James's great-great-grandaughter, Carol Holland. The staff at Crewe station remembered him when they gave his grandson Robert VIP treatment on a long wait at during World War One.

A letter from G.R. Thompson, chairman of the LNWR Society states: 'What is very evident is that with the lack of a State Retirement Pension [commenced 1908] people worked as long as they could in order to keep body and soul together…. If an engine-man had no other income than what he got from the Railway Company I cannot see him putting anything away for his old age'.

My cousin Forrest Hammersley, a railway enthusiast knowledgeable on railway history, finds it difficult to believe that James Cartlidge really worked for the railway. The premier historian of the line, Edward Talbot, concurred in a personal communication to me: 'I can offer no real explanation for what seems to be an erratic career.' In his study of the line, *LNWR Recalled*, he puts the problem more generally: 'As far as the LNWR was concerned, honest endeavour had no chance against influence posessed by other aspirants, as regards securing a reasonably remunerative post, early enough in life to appreciate it and give of one's best to its duties. Those who did so by the age of 30, and they were very few, had powerful "friends at court".'[289]

Officers of the LNWR Society have been unable to find any mention of Cartlidge in their records. Talbot notes that 'records of the service of all staff were kept in the Staff Registers. Each volume was a massive two thousand pages.'[290] These registers in conjunction with the GWR (Joint Staff Registers Cheshire RO NPR2/1-6 now on line — no Cartlidges) are currently held in the Cheshire Record Office and the name Cartlidge does not appear in them. A letter dated May 1993 from Diane Blackhouse, a research consultant employed by Cheshire County Council, states: 'A search was made of the nominal indexes to these three volumes [NPR2/1-3 c1869-c1892] but no reference was found to the name Cartlidge.' A personal check discovered that the first volume covering 1850-1868 is listed in the finding aid at Chester although the listing states that the volume does not exist. NPR2/1, the first available volume, commences 1869. No trace of the name has been found in the large number of LNWR records held at the P.R.O. at Kew.

Angela Houston, my professional researcher in London, considered the lack of documentation to be mysterious considering James's working life on the LNWR spanned the years 1861 or 1862 to 1909. Despite James having two brothers, three sons and a cousin who were

157

also known to be railwaymen, four of the six are documented as working for the LNWR.

William (born 1841) worked on the railway at Bushbury and Charles (born 1848) was killed in a LNWR accident at Spon Lane on 28th August 1866 and has a memorial plaque giving these details in St Mary's Church, Astbury. The 1881 census entry for Cecil Street Rushall[291] states that James was 'Night Foreman LNW railway', and James Robert Samuel, his second son living at home, was 'Fireman LNW Railway'. Albert his eldest son, now married, was also described as 'Fireman L&NW Railway Co'.[292] Leonard Cartlidge, a railway engine driver of Walton-on-the-Hill, Staffordshire, appears aged 34 in the 1901 census. Albert also became an engine driver. Reuben, described to me by Jean Cartlidge as 'not like the others', was a railway shunter. James had a first cousin, E.W. Cartlidge, who, according to *The Sentinel* newspaper in 1928, 'was for many years Stationmaster at Burslem' on the North Staffordshire Railway. His name does not appear in the appropriate register for the North Staffordshire Railway.

Talbot points us toward a possible explanation: 'The Carlisle post [of locomotive foreman] was invariably filled by someone with influential connections. Among those I recall were Trevithick, Homfry, Chambres … all these men were eventually promoted to Crewe'.[293] 'The chief at Crewe got £300 a year and was the second highest paid foreman on the line. The highest was Carlisle £350 a year … [for extra responsibilities] … despite all these extra duties he still had the title of "Locomotive Foreman". It was typical of the LNWR to use job titles which were out of alignment with responsibilities of the job, especially by comparison with other companies'.[294]

Influence in high places would seem a likely explanation for James's unconventional − and apparently officially undocumented – career with the LNWR. Was the name Cartlidge eliminated from the indices on instructions from high?

Poor Margaret, or the 'innocent victim' as Prosper Mérimée called her, died from 'senile decay and heart failure' on 22nd October 1910 at the age of sixty-nine. She would have been worn out through constant child-bearing, having given birth to at least seven sons and three daughters. On her death certificate James, as informant, is described as 'Railway Servant (retired)'.

* * *

Following Margaret's death a gap of four and a half years occurs in Eugénie's letters.

Eugénie's companion Isobel Vesey returned with the Empress from Constantinople on 30th July. The diaries of Miss Vesey were made available to Jasper Ridley who was kind enough to look at them again on my behalf. They apparently have a gap between 30th July 1910 until 2nd April 1913. Mr Ridley reported in a letter to me that he had seen nothing relating to October 1910, the month Margaret died.

There is however evidence of the Empress's state of mind a few days after Margaret's funeral. She was giving a presumably pre-arranged house party. Her guests were Comte Primoli, Lucien Daudet, the novelist's son who wrote about the weekend to his mother, and an unidentified couple, the 'Earles', of whom he said the Empress seemed very fond.[295]

Daudet wrote on 15th November that the day before the Empress had appeared for lunch looking tired and sad, complaining that she had coughed a lot in the night. When she suddenly decided to go to London, the two men hurriedly changed, and were rushed into her car. The three just caught the London train. On the journey their hostess was in reminiscent mood, speaking of old friends. Some, she said, were loyal and some were not. Daudet described the 84-year-old Empress 'looking beautiful as fate in her town clothes'. She took a taxi-cab to Maples where she did some shopping, 'chasing upstairs and downstairs', and eventually taking her escorts for a well-earned tea.[296] 'Primoli and I were done for!' wrote Daudet, yet the Empress had become high-spirited, as 'she needed physical agitation to calm her emotional turmoil'. Daudet believed that she was unrecognised all day. The following day, the 15th, was St Eugenia's Day, her own saint's day. She had spoken about it on the train journey home when eight people occupied their carriage for six, and recalled that Prince Napoleon ('Plon-Plon') had one year refused to propose her health on her saint's day at Compeigne on the pretext of being unable to extemporise.[297]

He assumed that the reason for her sadness was the memories stirred up by the recent marriage (on 10th November) of Prince Victor Napoleon Bonaparte and Princess Clementine of Belgium. He did not know — or was not revealing — that Margaret's death a few days earlier was responsible for his hostess's sadness.

* * *

The death of James Cartlidge occurred on 23rd February 1929, a week before his 92nd birthday.

He was buried with Margaret. Their private grave in a prominent position in Ryecroft cemetery is unmarked: we found it on our visit only thanks to a helpful attendant on duty, and because we had the grave number (21=2=29). The couple had produced nine known children, with many grandchildren and great-grandchildren to mourn their passing. This was a time when people set great store by such things as memorials to the dead. All the Cartlidges in James's direct line for the previous two hundred years have memorial stones standing today, as do his descendants on my husband's line. Could anonymity after death have been part of a pact of silence, or even a condition for a possible annuity for James? He made his will six months after his wife's death and 19 years before his own. It gave priority to funeral expenses and mentioned money in (unspecified) bank accounts to be divided between five of his sons. According to Jean Cartlidge, the widow of his grandson Robert, who knew him personally, James had enjoyed life in his latter years: 'He was a great sportsman, and he went every Saturday to the Walsall Hippodrome'.

The newspaper article about James, presumably from the only local Walsall paper of the time, the Walsall *Observer*, was returned to England by one of his half-brother's descendants in Canada. A nephew in Yorkshire sent us a copy. The only mention of Margaret, James's late wife, appears at the end of the text. The reporter appears to have mistaken James's reference to his wife's 'distant relation', an author named Pemberton (who would of course be Robert Pemberton) as meaning the adventure author Max, later Sir Max, Pemberton (1863-1950). Had Margaret Pemberton been a Pemberton by blood rather than by adoption, Robert Pemberton would have been her nephew – hardly a *distant* relation.

Albert, James's eldest child, married for the second time in October 1902. At that time he described his father as a railway foreman. On the death of his first wife the inquest reported Albert's occupation as engine driver with the Midland Railway. This may have been an error.

* * *

In the autumn of 2002 I received out of the blue a telephone call from Australia. It was from Heather, the granddaughter of Albert, who was delighted to have made contact with me through a lady researching the Pembertons, with the news that her father, Albert Douglas Pemberton Cartlidge (born 12th July 1914) is living in Australia. His father was married twice and there were no children of the first marriage, which accounts for A. Douglas's and his five sisters' late arrival.

James Robert Samuel, the second son who according to his elder son had 'an undue respect for authority', was a fireman with the LNWR at the age of 18, then worked for a while as asylum attendant and then as a Conservative Club manager. He was married on Christmas Day 1890 to Susan Helen Taylor, a schoolmistress. J. Robert S., or Robert as he preferred to be known, returned to his former employment and, as head attendant, spent the remainder of his working life at the County Asylum at Burntwood, Lichfield. Helen became mistress of the nearby Chorley School. After giving birth to five children, two dying as infants and one at the age of nine, she died in Stafford Asylum from 'melancholia and exhaustion' in 1908. In 1917 after living with a sister, Robert married 'Emmy' Gardner, head nurse at the Asylum, and retired two years later. The hospital presented them with a silver tea service to mark the occasion. James Cartlidge was a witness at the marriage in Burntwood. This was during World War One, and although eighty years of age, James was 'doing his bit' working in the village as a 'cow foreman', probably living with his son.[298]

J. Robert S. later spent many years at Norton Lindsey, a village about ten miles from Leamington Spa, the town where the royal train would halt in the early hours during Queen Victoria's journeys to Scotland and which the Empress visited whilst living in exile at Farnborough.

His second wife Emmy died in the 1930s. He later married Muriel Jobson, who outlived him.

By his first wife Helen, J. Robert S. had three sons: Robert, Eric Albert Pemberton, and John Robert who died in infancy; and two daughters, Margaret Elizabeth who died aged nine, and Margaret Helen who died in infancy. My husband, the son of Eric Albert Pemberton, a captain in the Royal Engineers who died in a road accident whilst on military service in 1942, is his only grandchild.

Aunt Jean (Jane Smith), born in 1891 and a Cartlidge by marriage, was until the arrival of the Internet my only primary source of Cartlidge history. A woman of very decided views, she did not encourage my researches, in the early stages telling me that her late husband's family reminiscences were 'a lot of silly nonsense'. Nevertheless she replied to my questions, telling something of what she remembered, although one or two details have proved inaccurate.

Margaret and James's firstborn Albert she described as 'a nice fellow'. Later information from Margaret Tinkler, the granddaughter of his brother Howard Victor, indicates that she was confusing Albert with Howard. Reuben, Jean said, was known as 'Carroty', his red hair having been confirmed by his grandson Dennis Victor. According to Jean, 'he was not like the others'. He had worked as a shunter on the railway and in later life was a shopkeeper. Reuben's descendants told me that 'Grandfather James' was a sometime 'Royal Porter'.

James and Margaret's eldest daughter Hannah Letitia ('Letty') was 21 years old on 9th October 1886 when the mysterious lady referred to only as 'H' paid a visit to the Empress at Farnborough. Could 'H' have been Hannah? On 8th September 1890 in Rushall, Letty married George Jackson Fisher, described as an 'engine driver'; the bride's father was described as a 'railway engine driv-

Hannah Letitia and her husband
George Jackson Fisher

er'. George later became a Walsall coal merchant.

According to Albert's son Douglas, Albert Sr gave Letty's husband financial help to expand his business. An e-mail dated 27th Jan 2003 from Douglas's daughter Heather states 'I certainly think from my father's description, that Albert was the sort of man that would keep his word to his dying day,' which Douglas confirmed to me when he visited England in May 2004.

In 1901 George and Letty Fisher were in Aston, Birmingham: 'She [Letty] was a small person — just like her mother', according to Aunt Jean. Eugénie and Margaret were both petite: 'Rosie's [the sister of the Empress' companion Miss Vesey] shoes were size three, but the Empress' boots were much too small for her.'[299] My husband remembers Letty, who kept a parrot, as a tiny but striking figure in a long black dress. Aunt Tish, as she was known to Reuben's family, was a music teacher and had two sons, Bert and Bob, and a daughter or grand-daughter Jackie, who was photographed in a Girl Guide's uniform (the Guides had been founded in 1910) alongside her grandfather James Cartlidge. Aunt Jean told me that Jackie married an Australian 'just before the war'.

Sara Jane Abigail, who sometimes signed her name as 'Abby', had a milliner's shop in Walsall prior to her marriage in September 1893 at Rushall to Alfred Brown, a tailor, the son of John Brown described as a gentleman.. Alfred Brown is listed as a widower of the Baker's Arms in 1901 [RG13/2703 p20].

Howard Victor was a pork butcher, beer retailer and keeper of the Walsall Union Inn. Reuben, the redhead, remained in the district where, after working on the LNWR, he became a shopkeeper. Only Albert, J. Robert S., Reuben, Jesse William, Howard Victor and Hannah Letitia are named in their father's will, which also mentions a niece, May Pemberton Cartlidge. Her brother

Douglas (born 1914) has identified May as his elder sister. May was to receive the picture of James's late wife should his daughter Hannah Letitia predecease him.

In 1901 Maria, as Margaret, was housekeeper to Jos Jenvey, a widower aged 50 with five young sons.[300] She has not been subsequently traced. Frederick evidently emigrated to America.

In 1910 Mary Cartlidge, a great-niece aged nine, born in Pennsylvania to an English father and Irish mother, was living with Letitia Pemberton, the daughter of Robert Sr from Leigh, in New Martinsville, West Virginia.

The 1930 census shows a Frederick Cartlidge, 54, with wife Maria, 57, both born in England, living at 219 Bert Avenue, Trenton, New Jersey.

* * *

The forebears of Joe Brindley of Astbury, who died in 1974 aged 87, took over Peel Farm, formerly the site of the Manor House of Newbold Astbury.[301] Joe appears to be related to the D. Brindley of Parr's Bank, Leigh, where Margaret and James were married. Joe told his neighbour Frank Cartlidge of his particular interest in French history of the nineteenth century. Might he have heard rumours of Margaret Cartlidge's story?

A well-known and easily recognisable miniature of the Empress turned up in a collection of miniatures owned by a Stoke-on-Trent resident shown on *The Antiques Road Show* in 1994. Neither the owner nor the experts appeared to be aware of the identity of the subject. Stoke-on-Trent is not very far from Walsall, where most of the Cartlidges lived. Had the miniature been in the hands of one of the family?

Aunt Jean was not in the habit of giving presents but she gave me – saying only, 'You should have these' – two

166

quite large, well-used fans which came from the house of her father-in-law, J. Robert S. Cartlidge. By referring to a specialist book, *Fans* by Nancy Armstrong, I have identified them as being Spanish, and of the 19th century. The carved wooden sticks are pine, from Cuenca.[302]

J.Robert S. had died in 1952, in his ninetieth year, long before the British public in any numbers went to Spain for their holidays. Were they inherited from his Spanish mother?

CHAPTER TWENTY-ONE

Eugénie: The End and the Enigmas

'The Empress will leave plenty of written material behind her since she always had a weakness for keeping letters, etc. There will be documents to elucidate the circumstances of her marriage, political paper in abundance.'
– Frédéric Loliée, Women of the Second Empire (1907)[303]

The Empress continued a close association with the younger members of the royal family who visited her often. She also entertained many illustrious people from the Continent. During the First World War Farnborough Abbey was turned into a convalescent home for officers. Eugénie still lived at the house and took a great interest in the patients and in the running of the home. The victorious end to the Great War gave her great satisfaction since she considered it to be retribution for the defeat of the Second Empire. She took into the mausoleum a copy of Treaty of Versailles and read the entire document aloud to her husband's tomb.[304]

In December of 1919 the Empress, then aged 93, left Farnborough Hill to winter at her Riviera home for the first time in six years. The following April she sailed from Marseilles to Gibraltar. After landing at Algeciras she travelled in her great nephew the 17th Duque de Alba's car to Seville and on 2nd May 1920 arrived at the Liria Palace in Madrid where she underwent a succesful operation for cataracts. Her nephew Alba was about to be married and Eugénie had offered Farnborough Hill for the reception. On 9th July he left for London to make preparations for the wedding. On Saturday 10th, after eating a good lunch Eugénie felt unwell, went to bed and died at 10am on Sunday 11th July 1920 after telling her attendants, 'The time has come for me to go away.'

Her body was returned to England. The stone coffin that she had carefully organised for her remains could not be found, and after a frantic search a substitute had to be arranged. This was too big for her chosen corner in the crypt of the mausoleum. It was raised with great difficulty to a very high ledge in a corner of the crypt, far above the remains of her husband and son. It is too high to be cleaned without a scaffold and it is impossible to place upon it any floral tribute.

* * *

E.A. Vizetelly records that Eugénie had her large collection of private papers presciently removed from the Tuileries.[305] So does Madame Carette: 'Prior to the siege Eugénie put papers on board the fleet, later they were sent to her in England.'[306] In Vizetelly's words, 'She had preferred to cast a veil over the past and even if the historical student should ever be privileged to consult her collection it is probable that this will only come to pass after an interval of many years.'[307]

169

Harold Kurtz, author of *The Empress Eugénie* (1964), in a reply to a letter from me in 1967 states that in her later life the Empress 'did a lot of paper burning, but not for personal reasons'. Kurtz had been told about her two safes and paper-burning but he could hardly know her reasons. Indeed, his own evidence points rather the other way.

Kurtz quotes a letter to 'someone who was familiar with the Empress's personal arrangements' from Princess Beatrice written on 13th July 1920: 'Knowing all your friendship for and connection with the dear late Empress's affairs I think you ought to know that all her correspondence with Mme. de Arcos was left by the latter to her niece. It seems to me that anyone who has the carrying out of the Empress's last wishes ought, if possible, to make sure that they are destroyed. The dear Empress was so particular about none of her correspondence, which must have been of a very intimate character, being kept that I think I ought to write to you on the subject.'[308]

In his book Kurtz asks 'What secrets of the past alarmed her?' and comments that 'the incendiary Princess [Beatrice] certainly showed great haste'. On his final page he writes '... none seems to have suffered so cruelly from interested detraction. In her lifetime she [Eugénie] helped the process by her lifetime refusal to combat libel.' Did not Mr Kurtz wonder why she would not answer back? He continues, 'Because of her proud Spanish faith in the ultimate justice of history, the libels persisted.'

In the foreword for *Napoleon III and Eugénie*, Jasper Ridley states 'His [Kurtz's] zeal for his heroine's reputation sometimes led him to supress and distort the facts.'[309]

How true.

Queen Victoria's eldest child, the Empress Frederick, surreptitiously returned the letters from her mother to England shortly before she died, although she had erased many of the pages. After Victoria's death in 1901, Princess Beatrice edited the queen's journals, laboriously copying them one by one, burning the originals as she went along. Her task took many years to complete. This editing distressed King George V and Queen Mary but they could not prevent it.[310]

Princess Beatrice was very close to Eugénie, and was quickly at her side after the news of her son's death. A close friend, if not the future fiancée, of the Prince Imperial, and although she subsequently married she died with his picture in her room. She was Eugénie's guest at Cap Martin in October 1901, the year Queen Victoria died. Certainly Beatrice would not have allowed anything to remain in her mother's journals which would have embarrassed the Empress.

In her will Eugénie states that no letters to her from sovereigns were to be published until fifty years after her death. There were surely letters from Victoria; where are they now? The Royal Archives Index on the website holds nothing about Empress Eugénie.

It is reasonable to ask whether Queen Victoria, after diligently and painstakingly writing up her diaries each night for the whole of her reign, really intended that posterity should be deprived of her original work. As for Empress Eugénie, there is an interesting insight into her sense of values through the reminicences of Leola, Duchess of Westminster. When writing of the engagement of her own parents: 'Backed up by Queen Victoria, everybody on both sides of the family forbade the engagement. In fact the only person who appears to have been sympathetic was the ex-Empress Eugénie, then living in retirement at Farnborough, who said to my father that she was glad to hear that his fiancée was beautiful, and that this was more important than being good – the world

Eugénie in Killarney in 1909,
accompanied by the Princesse de la
Moskowa

was chock full of good women but there were very few beautiful ones.'[311]

The Empress's will, made in England in September 1916, concerned her English affairs. (She prepared a Spanish one, dated June 1904.) Her English will is in duplicate, parts A and B, the reason stated on the document being that copy 'B' is prepared 'in the event of an accident to the first'. Version 'A' states: 'I confirm the pensions entered in the registers of Langlois and Fourchalt and Baring and Co. and those to persons and not to charitable works *and those which I suppress whilst leaving them a life annuity*." The words I have shown in italics are omitted in the attached 'duplicate' version 'B'. Another variation in version 'B' is an increase of 2,000 francs in each of the life annuities to the Duchesse de Mouchy and Princess Eugénie de la Moskowa.

My deduction is that Eugénie had given instructions that should the life annuity recipients 'which I suppress' have died before herself, version 'B' only of the will was to be used. There were probably instructions left that in this case version 'A' was to be destroyed. An 'accident to the first' (Version A) would seem highly improbable. Four thousand francs (about £412 in 1900) could be the amount of the suppressed annuities, which if the recipients had died would account for the increase of 2,000 francs in the annuities of Mouchy and Moskowa.

It would be most interesting to know who the recipients of the suppressed annuities were.

Dr. M. J. Orbell, the archivist for Barings, wrote in answer to my query in 1986: 'I imagine that the Baring and Co. to which The Empress referred in her will was ourselves, but I have been unable to find any relevant papers concerning pensions and life annuities paid by her and fear that none will have survived.' In 1985 John Orbell and L. S. Pressnell published a *Guide to the His-*

173

torical Records of British Banking, which states: 'Where a researcher wishes access to relatively recent customer records, than a bank might endeavour to obtain permission of the customer's successor before making any records available.'[312]

Farnborough Hill was left entailed according to English law. Eugénie said it was an 'important' house and should remain as it was when occupied, as a museum and memorial. Her wishes were not complied with. The law of entail was changed in 1925, and in 1926, after the death of Prince Victor Napoleon, trustees for his heir Prince Louis Napoleon Bonaparte (1914-1997) decided to sell the house in order to pay estate duties. Farnborough Hill became a boarding school for girls.

Following his death in May 1997, Louis Napoleon was suceeded by his elder son Charles Napoleon, born 1950. Interest in the Second Empire has never waned. Societies such as Les Amis de Napoleon III and the Academie de Second Empire revere its memory. There were moves afoot in France a few years ago and currently revived to return the remains of the Napoleon III to Paris. Possibly the recent renovation at Farnborough of St Michael's Abbey and the crypt which the Empress had not endowed will rescind this idea.

The Louvre Museum has recently redecorated and opened to the public the apartments Napoleon III used in the building. The cradle used by the infant Prince Imperial is on view along with several items of jewellery belonging to Empress Eugénie, including the coronet of pearls she wore for her wedding.

CHAPTER TWENTY-TWO

Conclusions

'Outside the Imperial entourage very little, probably nothing, is known of Her Majesty's private affairs. The administrator-general, Mons Pietri, is a monument of discretion.'
 – Edward Legge, The Empress Eugénie and Her Son (1910)[313]

"[The] descendants of a bastard should have as much right to discover their ancestors as those of legitimate descent."
 – Joy Lodey[314]

'Historians in general place far too much weight on written evidence.... [An historian] was quite shocked by the idea that he should watch a video of her [Mrs Thatcher] saying it. His unease vanished when I found a newspaper which quoted the remark. Once he saw it written down he accepted it as an historical fact.'
 – Brian Walden, Sunday Times, 23 August 1987[315]

'When researching history, you must use your imagination as well as facts.'
 – Asa Briggs[316]

Whether or not the Empress Eugénie had an illegitimate child is today a matter of little significance. The moral standards of her time were very different. If it had become known to the Emperor or to individuals close to him, it would have served as a lever upon Eugénie's decisions, or his, including some regarding matters of state. We cannot determine from the historical record whether such a lever was in fact applied. We can, however, strongly suggest that it existed.

The pattern of gaps and omissions, the unwitting testimony in the documentation, adds substance to the evidence instead of concealing it as was intended. The timescale of events in the lives of Eugénie and Margaret interlock. Their photographs show a similarity of features. Eugénie was petite in build and short in stature, as was Margaret.

Frank Cartlidge (born 1919), who was descended from the same family (John Cartlidge [1782-1860] and Mary) as Margaret's husband James, told me that all the Cartlidges he had known had mousy-coloured hair – none had red or black. (Susan) Helen, formerly Taylor, a daughter-in-law of Margaret, had light brown hair.[317] Her two sons Robert and Eric had, my husband recalls, jet-black hair, unusual in Englishmen. This would indicate that the black hair of the Cartlidge brothers was inherited through their father from Margaret, their Spanish grandmother. Photographs of both her son J. Robert S. and his elder son Robert reveal a bald patch on the hairline. A portrait of Pepe Alcañices, the likely father of Eugénie's daughter (see p.34), shows his luxuriant hair also parted in the centre with this identical hairline pattern. The same hairline can be seen in photographs of King Alfonso XII, Pepe's assumed son.

Eugénie was a redhead. This colour frequently jumps a generation, sometimes two. Margaret's hair colour is unknown, as her photographs are, of course, black and white. One of her sons, Reuben, was known as 'Carroty' because of his red hair. Eugénie's mother's husband, the Comte de Montijo, was a redhead. Her mother's lover who may have been her father, George Villiers (later Lord Clarendon), is reported to have had 'fair' or golden hair, which is open to various interpretations.

The opinion of some contemporary historians is that had Eugénie had a child her enemies would have found out. At the time of her marriage there was gossip about a child, and the Ambassador in Paris reported this story back to England. There was no proof since the little girl was safely hidden away in Manchester.

Napoleon III would have been informed of his wife's history. He acknowledged his own illegitimate sons, and in view of his lifelong womanising it is difficult to believe that he had only one recorded daughter, by Emily Brault, Mrs Gordon. This child is said to have died in infancy but she may, as often happened with illegitimate high-born girls, have been placed in a convent.

Eugénie's persistent reluctance to write her life story is suspect, as is her normally excellent memory failing to recall the year of her adventure in Spain. Her excursion with Pepe in the summer of 1840 was followed a few months later by the family troubles that so disturbed Prosper Mérimée. After this came her mother's journey, carrying a 'game basket' supposedly containing dahlia tubers, with 'Madame X' to the port of Bilbao where she then awaited Madame X's return. These events occur exactly at the likely dates of the conception, transportation, and registering of the child in England. Mérimée's letters to Eugénie's mother during 1840-1841 confirm this sequence and contain cryptic references to England and the county of Yorkshire, which adjoins Lancashire.

Mérimée regularly corresponded with Sutton Sharpe, his lawyer friend of Lincoln's Inn in London. Sharpe's home was in Nottingham Place near Regent's Park. The Church of St Martin-in-the-Fields was within walking distance of both his home and his place of work. Sir Henry Duckenfield, the Vicar at that time, had Leigh connections through his property in the district. His generous nature is recorded through a letter printed in *The*

Top left: James Robert Samuel Cartlidge and family. Below: Robert Cartlidge. Opposite top: the Prince Imperial, Eugénie's son. Opposite below: King Alfonso XII of Spain, who may well have been Pepe's son. Notice the similarities in the hairline.

179

Times shortly after his death, from someone calling himself 'PP': 'Duckenfield performed many acts of usefulness and benevolence.' Mérimée, Sharpe and Duckenfield form a tight link between Madrid, the home of Eugénie, and Leigh in Lancashire, where the Pembertons registered Margaret's birth.

According to Aunt Jean Cartlidge, her husband's and my father-in-law's paternal grandmother Margaret was Spanish but Robert and Betsy Pemberton, her 'parents', were both born in England. Robert Pemberton could write; the Wigan registrar recognised his signature, which appears on his family's birth and death certificates. This was unusual; many working people could read at this period but few could write. His literacy would be an advantage as a foster-father. In the 1840s the mail from Spain arrived in Manchester regularly each Monday.

Robert and Betsy had left the Leigh district between 18th May 1841, the day they registered Margaret's birth at Atherton Leigh, and 7th June 1841, census day, when they were found at Warrington, twelve miles away. This move was out of character with the custom of the day since the grandmother would care for the infant while the mother returned to work.

Robert's next known address is in 1846, in Barton-upon-Irewell, five miles from Atherton, Leigh, and the same distance from central Manchester.

When still very young Eugénie had an arrangement with her dentist Dr Evans that he would secretly send presents and money saved 'through her own economies' to some poor Spanish emigrants. Generosity, and for that matter economy, is out of her character. Surely the 'poor Spanish emigrants' were her little daughter and the foster parents. A letter of Lord Clarendon's dated 15th October 1841, five months after Margaret's birth states that he has just received two letters from Mrs Evans. Was this

Mrs Evans the Parisian dentist's wife? Correspondence between the educated classes was regular and prolific, and contained much gossip. Clarendon, who may have been her father, always took an interest in Eugénie but in view of Madame de Montijo's foolish reaction to his marriage, it is not surprising that she did not ask for his help in 1840.

Eugénie's highly emotional letter written to her future brother-in- law in May 1843 was shortly before Betsy Pemberton's anticipated death from consumption. This letter has received various interpretations by earlier biographers. It seems that the news from England had revived her traumas of two years earlier.

Margaret's lack of wealth has been cited as evidence against her aristocratic origins. Had the twelve-year-old child or her carers suddenly become rich when her natural mother married the Emperor, they would have attracted attention. In obscurity they were no threat. The Empress evidently pondered the morality of the situation, since after leaving Manchester in 1860 and witnessing the straitened circumstances in which Margaret lived, she asked her brother-in-law, 'Do you not think one asks too much of children?'

She would have been bound to ask for perpetual silence.

Eugénie had expected that the Emperor's proposal would make her beloved Pepe jealous and that he would marry her. Sadly disillusioned, she made the best of things and accepted the Emperor. Before the formal announcement of the engagement was made she sent the news to her sister and told her that she was worried about 'anonymous letters and tiresome things of that sort'. Mérimée, who was disturbed about the marriage, was afterwards asked — indeed, almost blackmailed — by the Imperial couple to edit the archives.

Paca, her sister, died in 1860. In her distress, an overwhelming desire to see her daughter was for the mourning Eugénie perfectly natural. Her 'holiday' to England and Scotland in dark and dreary November 1860, was injudicious and many people thought that she was unbalanced. Her entourage would have been carefully selected for their discretion. Her daughter was the 'succour' that her old friend Mérimeé, in his usual cryptic fashion, stated that she required.

It is obvious that after leaving Glasgow the pretext of going on to Liverpool was cover for Manchester, her real destination. On her arrival the first outing of the supposedly sick Empress was a visit to cotton-weaving shed. Margaret had worked as a weaver before her marriage and evidently her mother wished to see conditions for herself. The local press recorded her daytime movements in great detail.

A local diarist recorded these particular days as the darkest he had ever known and lights were left burning all day. Despite these dreary surroundings and her official mourning, the press reported her happiness on leaving Manchester and her smiling face when alighting at Leamington. Her smiles abruptly turned to depression after hearing, in the Catholic Church on Sunday 2nd December, the Rev. Davies' 'able and impressive discourse on the subject of the last judgement'. On her return to her hotel it was reported that she looked very pale and careworn.

There was a rapid change of plan and Eugénie left Leamington on Sunday at 2.56pm instead of staying until Monday or Tuesday as pre-arranged. Still in a state of emotional turmoil she visited Queen Victoria at Windsor on 4th December. Her Majesty wrote the next day to her daughter Vicky, 'I fear some great sorrow is preying upon her'.

In July 1867 after crossing the channel, the Empress had made a secret detour on the English mainland before visiting the Queen at Osborne House on the Isle of Wight. Lord Clarendon had known that she was 'going elsewhere'. Mérimée in his usual cryptic manner wrote to his friend Panizzi in London that the Empress was to spend a day incognito in London concerning her life with '*vos parages*', which is open to various interpretations. Panizzi was told to keep this information to himself and not write it down. Did Eugénie meet Margaret who was, unusually, not pregnant at that time? Or was the detour to meet Lord Clarendon?

The story reported by David Duff of an illegitimate relation, whose identity was secret, boarding the Royal train in the early hours at Leamington is significant. It is in character for the queen to have assisted her 'dear sister' and travelling companion to conveniently meet her daughter in the privacy of the royal train. Between 1876 and 1900 Margaret was conveniently living about 30 miles along the railway from Leamington. During that same time a young girl saw the Empress in Wolverhampton, very close to Margaret's home, in a district with a hotel and coach-house.

According to Agnes Carey, a mysterious lady described merely as 'H' visited the Empress at Farnborough on 9th October 1886. Everyone else in the book was named. Margaret's eldest daughter was Hannah Letitia, who had celebrated her 21st birthday earlier that year.

During the period of the Second Empire the Imperial couple founded the Eugénie and Napoleon Home. 'Inmates were given a small dowry to enable them to marry or to take up a business of their own choosing'.[318] Most of Margaret's children ran their own business at some stage in their lives Did they receive a similar dowry? If so, they would be unaware of its source.

Eugénie's last English will, written after Margaret's death, refers to annuities that she stated she repressed. Was Margaret's widower James Cartlidge amongst the recipients? Already retired when his wife died, he made his last will afterwards, nineteen years before his death in 1929. He instructed that money in any banks was to be divided amongst five of his sons, namely Albert, James Robert Samuel, Howard, Jesse William and Reuben. His daughter Hannah Letitia was to receive the photograph of his late wife. He had resources, yet his and his wife's grave has no memorial and is unmarked, unlike those of most other members of his line for two hundred years. At his death he left very little, but considering his great age and his circumstances it is remarkable that he left anything at all.

No explanationas have emerged as to how or why James Cartlidge left his farm work near Manchester and so rapidly gained apparently preferential employment, initially at Bushbury, close to the sidings where the royal trains so conveniently halted. The London and North Western Railway staff registers have no reference to the name of Cartlidge even though many members of the family, including James, are known and documented – including on a memorial plaque in Astbury church – to have worked for the company.

It appears that only the elder children of Margaret and James were privy to the family secret of a Spanish grandmother, since none of the descendants of the younger ones know anything of the story. My husband's uncle Robert Cartlidge (born July 1891), the first-born of Margaret and James's second son J. Robert S. (born 17th August 1862), was a generation older than his cousins including Albert Douglas who visited me, and this would account for Robert's evidently unique knowledge of their grandmother's Spanish origins.

(Albert) Douglas Pemberton Cartlidge was born in 1914. His father's first marriage had produced no children but his second wife, who he married in 1902, gave birth to five daughters and one son. Douglas, as he is known, told us of an occasion in the 1920s when he was instructed to dress smartly for an expected visit by two brothers from America. They were relatives and barristers, but they did not turn up. His daughter Heather who was present recalled her mother also relating the story, which she believed may have originated with Douglas's sisters, adding that the visitors were Pembertons.

Sarah Jane Pemberton had married a lawyer, William McGregor Hall, and their son Leonard was also a lawyer. The Empress had died in 1920. Did they visit England for a sight of her will?

Ethyl Smyth, the Empress's confidante, quoted her as saying: '[Eugénie] could not write her memoirs because people [Pepe?] in a moment of infidelity failed you, who could show them up but memoirs [would be] useless if this was not done'.

* * *

Eugénie's replies to a quiz in a 'confession book', a pastime of her day:

Your favourite trait in a man?
'Determination to do right even if it involves personal sacrifice'.
What would you have liked to be?
'Unknown and happy'.
Your favourite motto?
'Always do what is right, let the consequences be what they may'.[319]

* * *

185

What is the feeling within my immediate family, who, unlike myself, are directly involved as Margaret's descendants, regarding the results of my researches? For them, discovering an empress as an ancestor is no particular reason for excitement. My husband has no time for her. My daughter Caroline feels that as a young girl Eugénie was a high-spirited and interesting character but as Empress, she regards her as a political meddler who should have let well alone. She holds her largely responsible for the tragic fates of the erstwhile Emperor Maximilian and Empress Carlotta of Mexico. My son merely takes an academic interest in my researches and the discoveries I have made.

As for myself, there is the interesting coincidence of Eugénie's birth and my own occurring a century apart, almost to the hour. Whenever the date or her age is given in her life story, I can relate to my own circumstances at an equivalent date a century later. Perhaps this enables me to 'get under her skin' and understand her emotions and motivation at various stages in her life. Any mother will understand her anger and resentment at being parted from her daughter and her very strong although perhaps selfish need to keep in touch with her.

Class distinctions and moral attitudes during the nineteenth and early twentieth century were hypocritical by today's standards. It is unfair to judge the Empress Eugénie by the standards of today. It would have been impossible for Eugénie to acknowledge her secret family although inevitably there would have been those in her immediate circle and many people in Spain, including Miss Flower, Lucas and Don Carlos who were part of her mother's household, who knew of her past.

Margaret's circumstances would be difficult to live with. She had to keep the secret, although it would appear that her second son J. Robert S. and presumably her eldest, Albert, and possibly her daughter Hannah Letitia were aware of it. The Empress appears to have kept in touch and even visited on occasions convenient to herself. She does not emerge as a generous woman, but even had it been her nature she could not be liberal with financial help since this would attract unwelcome attention to the Cartlidges and speculation as to its source. Margaret, although the wife of a comparatively well-paid railwayman, had a very hard life of constant childbearing.

How different everything would have been had Pepe married her mother.

APPENDIX I

The Letters

Prosper Mérimée wrote frequently to Madame de Montijo between the summers of 1840 and 1841. Those letters which have been published have proved invaluable in this research. Those he wrote to the Comtesse at the time of her daughter's engagement to the Emperor and selected ones at the time of the supposed death of Paca's first-born appear to have been destroyed or repressed, probably by the Empress herself. Madame de Montijo's replies, according to Primoli, were burned in Mérimée's house fire. Sencourt, on the other hand, refers to them as a source which he says is from unpublished letters in the Alba Archives.

Prosper Mérimée's biographer says: 'There can be little doubt that mother and daughter consulted Mérimée in this situation; there can be little doubt too that he was opposed to the idea of a possible marriage, though the letters he must have written at the time to Mme de Montijo at that time were later destroyed by the Empress'.[320] A note at the bottom of the page states that 'the sequence of letters makes it clear that no very substantial part of the correspondence can have been burnt.'

Two hundred and sixty-one letters written by Eugénie were published after her death. They cover the period from 1836 to 1915. Her grand-nephew the 17th Duque de Alba evidently censored them prior to involving his joint editor, an academic, Gabriel Hanotaux. The latter comments in the preface of the collection that there was not a single letter in the archives of the Liria Palace (Alba's home) for the period between 1839 and 1843.[321] The sequence of the letters varies; an isolated one dated May 1843 (the only letter between 1838 and 1849) has puzzled earlier biographers who have put various interpretations upon it. They could not know that it was written at the time the news would have been received in Madrid of the imminent death from consumption of Betsy Pemberton, the illegitimate baby's foster mother. Eugénie was in a highly emotional state and her letter is full of self-pity. Between 27th May 1843 and 20th October 1843 there is a gap in published letters to Madame de Montijo from Prosper Mérimée.

The 54 known critical events in the lives of Margaret and her large family always coincide with a gap in the sequence of the available letters. For example, two were printed for May 1910, and Margaret died on 22nd October that year. The very next letter is dated November 1914. Likewise, letters from the periods of the thirteen important events in the lives of Eugénie's beloved Pepe Alcañices, his wife and his supposed son by Queen Isabella are sparse. Pepe married in April 1868. Eugénie mentioned him in a letter to her sister on 25th January that year. The next letter to be published is dated 23rd May. Pepe's wife died on 9th August 1896. Only two letters of Eugénie's appear for that year, written in April and May. Pepe died in December 1909 and just one of Eugénie's letters is known from that year, from 27th August. The next letter to be printed is dated 8th May 1910.

By the law of averages some of the dates of these 261 published letters would have coincided with the dates of the 54 notable occasions (births, marriages and deaths) had the choice been entirely random. (See the Table of Comparative Dates on pp. 194–195.) The printed list (dated 1953) of the contents of the Alba Archives gives an 'Archivo particular de la Emperatriz Eugenia, 1853–1920' – excluding, but not too pointedly, the critical early years 1840–1841.

Mérimée's letters to Sutton Sharpe, the English laywer, are deposited with a small file of Sharpe's papers in University College London. Those written by Mérimée do not include any for the period 1840-1841. None of Sharpe's replies to him are available between 1836 and October 1842. Sharpe was the likely link between Madame de Montijo and the child's foster parents, most probably through the good offices of the Rev. Duckinfield.

Mérimée's letters to the Laborde family follow the same pattern: one to Madame Alex de Laborde dated September 1838, followed by two to Leon Laborde dated (presumably by a third party) 'about 1840', and then the next bears the date 2nd May 1842. The introduction by Maurice Parturier to these letters claims, 'Here are all the letters' and in the next breath repeats the now familiar story; he goes on to say '1837–48, no longer exist'.[322]

Hector Bolitho, editor of Prince Albert's letters to his brother, says in the introduction to the book that much of the correspondence which covers the Prince's life is 'purely personal and therefore limited in its public interest'.[323] No letter written between 2nd November 1852 and 26th February 1853, the period of Eugénie and Napoleon's courtship, engagment, and marriage is published. Nor is any letter written between 13th October 1860 and 21st March 1861, bracketing the time of the Empress's mystery journey in November 1860. Given that following her sojourn in Manchester she went, in a very distressed state, to lunch with the Prince and Queen Victoria, Prince Albert's comments would have been interesting.

At the time of the Emperor's marriage Queen Victoria sent Lady Augusta Bruce, her mother's lady-in-waiting, to Paris 'as her observer'. Lady Augusta, no stranger to the city, would stay at her mother's Paris home or with her old friend Mary Clarke, now Madame Mohl. Lady Augusta's mother and Mary Mohl were hosts to many important and interesting people including Prosper Mérimée and Eugénie's aunt and uncle de Lesseps. It was at the Mohl's house that Lady Augusta met Dean Stanley, whom she married. The bride was of course the main topic of conversation in the French capital. She was not a popular choice for Empress, and the gossips had discovered that she had a child. The British Ambassador had recorded this in a dispatch to London.

In 1927 Lady Augusta's nephew Albert Baillie, Dean of Windsor, edited and published some of his aunt's letters. 'The letters were confidential and respect for the writer obliged me to honour that confidence ... Many of them are thrilling to me but are of no public concern'. Baillie published nothing written by his aunt at the time of the imperial engagement and marriage. A magnificent occasion – the marriage of an Emperor to a beautiful be-jewelled bride in the imposing setting of the highly decorated and candle-lit cathedral of Notre Dame – surely the most spectacular of the period. Would Lady Augusta, who was present, not consider this worthy of mention? Baillie comments on his aunt's writing about a bride he does not see fit to identify. 'There in all the tremulous excitement of a bride appears someone whom I remember as a sad old woman.' He would remember Eugénie, who had died seven years before as an old woman. Baillie published no letter written by his aunt at the time of the downfall of the Second Empire and the Empress's flight from Paris.

The letters of Julius and Mary Mohl contain none written at the time of the marriage. There is one from

Paris dated December 1852, followed by two undated ones written to 'Minnie and Hilly'. The next is dated 23rd October 1853. The letters confirm the very close relationship between Madame Mohl and Lady Augusta and Mme Mohl's intimate friendship with Mérimée. They prove the Mohls' intense dislike of Louis Napoleon and his regime, albeit Madame Mohl refers to her intimate friendship with the Emperor's foster sister Madame Cornu. Louis Fagan, editor of the letters, writes: 'Mme. Mohl was a good hater ... the most distinguished and cultivated men in France shared her enmity against Louis Napoleon and enjoyed more than ever meeting each other.'[324]

* * *

The Villiers (Clarendon) collection of letters deposited in the Bodleian Library, Oxford, contains none written between 14th February 1841 and 5th October 1841. (Eugénie's baby would have been born in May 1841). There appear to be no letters deposited in the library which make any reference to Eugénie's trip to Scotland and Manchester in 1860.

Clarendon's letters (edited by Maxwell) contain none written at the time of the engagement and marriage of Eugénie, his former mistress's daughter, to his own close friend Louis Napoleon — hardly an everyday event by any standard! His letters to Teresa, his sister, are dated 19th December 1852 and 27th December 1852; then follows a gap until after the imperial engagement and marriage in January. The next letter is dated 8th March 1853. Clarendon's letters to his wife that have been deposited in the Bodelian are dated 18th, 27th and 30th December of 1852 and 6th, 19th, 20th and 25th January of 1853, seemingly breaking the pattern. Yet none of them make any reference whatsoever to this important marriage!

However, a catalogue in the Bodleian Library lists 'a draft of an UNDATED letter "from Clarendon to ? giving advice on ?'s marriage to 'B'.'[325] The first few pages of this extremely long and difficult-to-read letter leads to the belief that what has been previously deciphered and indexed as 'B' is in fact 'N3', or a reference to Napoleon III written in a form of shorthand:

For example: 'It is N3's wish as well as your own to have the opinion of a friend….' 'Feeling however very sure that it is N3's position and … is the alarmed contingency that mainly occupies your mind' 'The marriage of N3 with anyone [upon whom his?] choice falls must excite the opinion of the world' 'an honourable and intellectual calling levels all distinction of rank'. Further study of this letter could prove illuminating since it may well prove to be a reply to Eugénie, who had written to her old friend (or father) of her misgivings about her forthcoming marriage. Lord Clarendon died on 27th June 1870; a letter of Eugénie's was dated dated 12th May 1870, and the next one to be published is dated November 1870.

The Comtesse des Garets states that she witheld from publication certain letters (no dates given) written to her by her mistress the Empress, because of their intimate passages of 'vital affection and maternal solicitude'.[326] Such emotions are surely not to the letter-writer's discredit. The suppression of these letters creates speculation as to the identity of the object of this maternal solicitude and affection.

The Alba Archives in Madrid holds nine reports of a series covering Eugénie's regency year, 1859. One report, number five, for the period 5th-12th June is missing.[327] This was the summer when Margaret Pemberton was involved in a love affair. She married on 16th October 1859 and her first child was born exactly six months later, 16th April 1860. There is no indication as to whether these reports contain anything of a personal nature.

The diaries of Isobel Vesey, Eugénie's companion in her later life, have been made available to Jasper Ridley. They have a gap between 30th July 1910 and 2nd April 1913. Following my enquiry, Mr Ridley reports in a personal letter to me that he was able to look again and has nothing relating to October 1910, the month Margaret died.

The Empress Frederick, 'Vicky', the eldest child of Queen Victoria, returned the letters her mother had written to her to England, shortly before she herself died. 'Occasionally whole pages are rendered undecipherable with erasures. This must have been her work'.[328] The dates of the erasures could give an indication as to their content, particularly when compared with the regular letters Vicky received from her mother.

Dates and Letters

Here follow the forty-one critical dates in the life of Margaret Pemberton and her children, correlated with Eugénie's known correspondence. A further eight, following the same pattern, are added from information given by Margaret Tinkler, née Cartlidge, granddaughter of Howard Victor. Two more were passed on by Heather née Pemberton Cartlidge, granddaughter of Albert.

EVENT	DATE	EUGÉNIE'S LETTERS
Birth of Margaret	circa 4th May 1841	None between 1839 and the 1843 impassioned letter
	The next letter is not dated until 1849	
Death of Betsy	25th June 1843	One letter dated 16th May
Albert conceived	July 1859	no letter after June 28th
Margaret married	16th Oct 1859	no letters after June 1859
Margaret's 20th birthday	4th May 1860	no letters April 18–May 16th
Margaret's 21st birthday	4th May 1862	no letters at all for 1862
Margaret's 30th birthday	4th May 1871	no letters at all for 1871
Margaret's 40th birthday	4th May 1881	1 letter July 1881
Margaret's 50th birthday	4th May 1891	no letters 1891
Margaret's 60th birthday	4th May 1901	no letters between Jan–Aug
Charles, James's brother, died LNWR accident	28th August, 1866	no letter after July 1866
Albert born	16th April 1860	gap 18th Apr–16th May
Albert baptised	13th May 1860	
Albert married.	1880- April 1881	no letter Jan1880–July 1881
Albert 2nd marriage	11th Oct. 1902	no letter after June 1902
James R. S. born.	17th Aug. 1862	no letters that year
James R. S. married	25 Dec. 1890	1 letter 18th June
Hannah Letitia born	9th Dec 1864	1 letter 24th Aug
Hannah L. married	July-Sept 1890	1 letter dated 18th June
Howard Victor baptised	May 1867	no letters that year
Howard Victor married	July-Sept 1894	no letters that year
Sara Ann Abigail born	12th July 1869	no letters 1869
Sara Ann Abigail married	25th Sept.1893	2 letters dated Apr.'93.
Maria Margaret Ellen b.	April 1872	2 letters 1872: 1 Jul; 16 Nov
Frederick Charles born	4 May 1874	no letter 5th Apr– 28th Sept
Jesse Wm born	13 Dec 1876	no letter after 6th April
Jesse Wm died	12th April 1917	no letters 1917
Reuben born	4th June 1878	no letter 8th Apr–26th June
Reuben married	Mar–June 1897	no letter 1st Mar–22nd Oct
Sydney Doctor born	July 1880	2 letters: 23rd Jan; 11th May
Sydney died	April, 1881	no letter until July 1881

Albert 1st marriage	16th Oct. 1880	2 letters 1880: 23 Jan; 11 May
James Robert Samuel m.	25th Dec. 1890.	1 letter 18th June
Robert his first son born.	July 1891	no letters 1891
Margaret Eliz. born	Oct-Dec 1895	no letters 1895
Eric Albert Pemberton born	17th Dec 1899	no letters 1899
Margaret Eliz died.	Oct-Dec 1904	no letters 1904
John Robert born/died	Sept 1/4 1905	no letters 1905
Margaret Helen born & died	1906	no letters 1906
Helen (wife of JRS) died	27th Oct 1908	1 letter 19th Feb, Kandy
M and J's golden wedding	Oct 1909	1 letter 1909 dated Aug 27th
Margaret died	24th Oct 1910	2 letters 1910, dated May
	The very next letter is dated November 1914	

From Margaret Tinkler grandaughter of Howard Victor Cartlidge:

Howard Victor C. married	28th July 1894	No letters 1894.
Margaret Elizabeth born	10th May 1895	No letters 1895.
Dorothy Eleanor born	April 14th 1896	1 letter 24 Apr from Cap Martin
George Howard born	31st July 1897	1 letter March, 1 letter October

For 1898 there are 18 letters published:

Florence Anne born	1899	No letters 1899
Dorothy Eleanor married	16th April 1917	No letters 1917
Her husband died in action	May 1917	No letters 1917

From Albert Douglas Pemberton Cartlidge:

Albert (firstborn) 2nd m.	11th Oct 1902	No letters after June
Albert Douglas born	12th July 1914	1 letter 24th Nov
Robert Pemberton died	28th Sept. 1897	Letters 1 Mar and 22 Oct

196

APPENDIX II

Burgoyne letter

Ryde
Sept 13

My dear Robert

We were very much amused at your letter especially as in my desire to deceive the telegraph clerks at Portsmouth. I deceived you also

Any how was it not an odd thing that we should have been at Deauville and have been of much use to H.J.M. On Tuesday at about noon I was at desk doing something or other and two strangers came on board and asked to see the yacht. I shewed them over & he then bluntly told me he was commissioned by H.J.M. to ask me to to take her on board under the protection of the British flag and take her to any port in England. I went to the Empress myself and told her I expected bad weather, she told me it was imperative that she should leave France at once. I told her I would do all I could, but she must expect heavy weather and much discomfort. Lord knows they got it poor things, we had a strong wind for four hours & then the wind chopped round NW and a very heavy head sea got up however without boring you with details of a yacht voyage, the Gazelle behaved much better than one would have supposed she would have done − at about ¼ to 3 (not 3.55am 8-7 as the papers say) we left for our anchor in Ryde − After a consultation with Amy I agreed the condition that I should change all and every detail getting her Majesty aboard and I told these "strangers" to meet me at a place on the quay at 11 at night − I sent a card with a message asking Her Majesty to put trust in me giving a pledge as an English "Sailor" that I would get her safely across Channel. I made all my preparations and at 11.30pm received a visit from a young [unclear] who was kind enough to bring "a fast friend who had just arrived from Paris" and who wanted to [unclear] an English yacht. Of course this was a spy, so I showed no dint of reserve and shewed him all I could, mentally wishing I had him three leagues off the coast, but away they went and at 5 min after 12 midnight the Empress came up to me and in the nicest and most charming manner introduced herself to me in wonderfully good English. I took her arm and we walked on board. She was very much agitated, and going over the side I remarked, N'avez pas peur, Madame" She replied, I am quite safe with an English Gentleman − She then went below and Amy gave her some coffee & c & gave them all the latest news.

At 6am I cast loose from the quay & at 7 the pilot came on board, & we sailed out. I ought to say that the weather looked <u>awful</u> although the wind was fair, & the Barom. was falling.

Anything more charming than the poor Empress I never saw so kind and so sorry to give trouble she never ceased to tell me that she was much impressed with Amy, and informed me I ought to think myself lucky to have such a wife.

We had a sad day today the Admiralty sent over at Mrs Hughes' express wish all the men saved in the Captain's Launch − it utterly upset me to see the grief these loyal fellows showed at meeting their Captain's Wife − she is perhaps too calm, & appears to be very uneasy if Amy for whom she has a great attachment leaves her for even short a time. A large portion of her men are Portsmouth men and the distress to those belonging to them will be frightful.

I had such a nice letter from old Sir John today, fancy his being able to write at all at such a moment – Gazelle went on to her mud bed for the winter today – Best love to all.

Believe me

Yours very truly

J Montague Burgoyne

(Original formatting, spellings and punctuation have been preserved as much as possible.)

Notes

INTRODUCTION

1   Brett, M.V., and Brett, Oliver, eds., *The Journals and Letters of Viscount Esher*, vol. 3, p. 263.

2   Legge, Edward, *The Empress Eugénie and Her Son*, p. 307.

3   Mostyn, Dorothy, *Farnborough Hill. The Story of a House*.

4   Reid, Michaela, *Ask Sir James*, p. 269.

5   Kurtz, Harold, *The Empress Eugénie*, p. 343.

6   Smyth, Dame Ethyl, *Streaks of Life*, p. 15.

7   Barker, Nancy N., *Distaff Diplomacy*, p. 125.

8   Vizetelly, Ernest Alfred [as 'Le Petit Homme Rouge'], *The Court of the Tuileries*, p. 162.

9   Kurtz, p. 384.

10   Tschudi, Clara, *Eugénie Empress of the French*, p. 161.

11   Murat, Princess Caroline, *My Memoirs*, p. 163. Princess Murat died in 1903. Her book was published in the lifetime of the Empress, in 1910.

CHAPTER ONE: Eugénie: The Beginning

12   Zeldin, Theodore, *France 1848-1945: Ambition, Love and Politics*, p.106. Quoted in Thea Thompson, *Edwardian Childhoods*, p.4.

13   Ridley, Jasper, *Napoleon III and Eugénie*, p. 140.

14   Duff, David, *Eugénie and Napoleon III*, p. 62.

15   Villiers, George, *A Vanished Victorian*, p. 41.

16   Duff, pp. 62-63; Maxwell, Sir Herbert, *Life and Letters of Lord Clarendon*, p. 180.

17   Clarendon Letters, Folio No. 63, Bodleian Library, Oxford.

18   Clarendon Papers, MS Eng. lett d 515, Bodleian Library, Oxford.

19   Parturier, Maurice, ed., *Correspondence Générale de Prosper Mérimée* [hereinafter cited as CG], Vol. XX, p. 100.

20   Raitt, A. W., *Prosper Mérimée*, p. 164.

21   Ibid., p. 367.

22   Sergeant, Philip W., *Last Empress of the French*, p. 27.

23   CG, July 1853, p. 100
24   Pers. comm. with Brian Little of Eugénie House, Clifton.
25   Kaye, M.M., ed., The Golden Calm, pp. 53-54.
26   Hanotaux, Gabriel, and Alba, Jacobo, 17th Duke of, eds., *Lettres Familières de L'Impératrice Eugénie* [hereinafter cited as LF], notes vol 2. p. 234.
27   Kurtz, p. 17.
28   Named in the will of the Condesa de Montijo.
29   Ridley, p. 149.
30   Ibid., pp. 149-151.

CHAPTER TWO: Margaret: Beginnings

31   Eugénie's mother's brother William Escott Kirkpatrick married Eliza Ann Parkinson, the eldest daughter of a Jeremiah Parkinson. ref. C. Carlin. There is no apparent connection.
32   Lunn, John, *History of Atherton*, pp. 243, 262.
33   Letter from 'PP' to the editor of *The Times*, 28th Jan 1858.
34   Wetzel County W.V. Obituaries, Vol. 2, p. 82.

CHAPTER THREE: Eugénie: The Missing Year

35   Bicknell, Anna, *Life in the Tuileries*, p. 195.
36   Kurtz, p. 184, quoting Madame Bouvet.
37   Lecture by the 17th Duke of Alba at Oxford, 5th Jun 1941. Ridley gives Oxford only.
38   Garets, Marie, Comtesse des, *The Tragic Empress*, p. 217.
39   Primoli, Count Joseph, 'L'enfance d'une souveraine', *Revue des Deux Mondes*, VII:17, pp. 752-788.
40   Martineau, Henri, ed., *Correspondence de Stendhal* vol. 3 p37 (French Edition p. 576)
41   *Correspondence de Stendhal*, vol. 3, p. 374 (French edition, p. 576.)
42   Alba, Oxford lecture, pp. 4-5.
43   Higham, Charles, *Errol Flynn: The Untold Story*, p. 63.
44   Sencourt, Robert [Robert Esmond Gordon George], *The Life of the Empress Eugénie*, p. 43. (French version, p. 40.)
45   Martineau, vol. 3, p. 583.
46   Sencourt, p. 43. (French version, pp. 39-40.)
47   Alba, Jacobo, 17th Duke of, Lecture at Barcelona University, *Boletin de la Real Academia de Historia*, CXX, pp. 71-101. Madrid 1947
48   Mérimée, Prosper, *Lettres a la Famille Delessert*, p. xxv.

49   University College London 81/4-113.

50   Garets, p. 180.

51   Chapman-Huston, Desmond, and Baviera, Princess Pilar de, *Alfonso XIII*, p. 10.

52   Llanos y Torriglia, Félix de, *Maria Manuela Kirkpatrick*, p. 131, also Eugenia de Guzman Villa Urritia p. 48.

53   Petrie, Charles, *The Spanish Royal House*, p. 186.

54   Sencourt, p. 350.

55   Kurtz, p. 316.

56   Alba, Oxford lecture.

57   Fulford, Roger, ed., *Dearest Child: Letters between Queen Victoria and the Princess Royal*, p.8.

58   Culpeper, Nicholas, *Herbal and English Physician*, 1826 re print 1981, p 222.

59   Grieve, Margaret, *A Modern Herbal*, p. 397

60   Fleury, Maurice, Comte de, *Memoirs of the Empress Eugénie*, vol. 1, p. 12.

61   Grieve, p. 381.

62   CG, vol. 2, p. 445

63   David Duff, *Eugénie and Napoleon III*, page 67.

64   CG, vol. 2, p. 445

65   CG, vol. 2, p. 448

66   CG, vol. 2, p. 475

67   A.W. Raitt, Prosper Mérimée, p. 35

68   Martineau, vol. 3 p. 583.

69   CG, vol. 2, page 479.

70   CG ,vol. 9, page 96 footnote 1

71   CG, vol. 3, p. 2

72   CG, vol. 3, p. 23

73   Felix de Llanos y Torriglia. Maria Manuela Kirkpatrick. p.74

74   Lecture Barcelona Boletin del la Real Academia de Historia, CXX 78.

75   Review des deux Mondes V11(xvii) 752.88), Paris, Oct. 1923)

76   Ethyl Smyth, Streaks of Life, page 32

77   CG, vol. 3, p. 29

78   CG, vol. 2, p. 345

79   CG, vol. 3, p. 34

80   CG, vol. 3, p. 35

81   CG, vol. 3, p. 32

82   CG, vol..3, p. 46

83   CG, vol. 3, p. 49

84   CG, vol. 3, p. 49

85 CG, vol. 3, p. 36
86 Anna Bicknell, *Life in the Tuileries*. pp 73–4
87 CG, vol. 3, p. 51
88 CG, vol. 3, p. 59

CHAPTER FOUR: Margaret: Without a Mother

89 Ford, Richard, *Gatherings from Spain*, p. 243.
90 CG, March 1855 p. 454
91 CG
92 CG, April 1843 p. 357
93 Personal communication from Dr. A. R. L. Clark.
94 Wetzel County W.V. Obituaries, vol. 3.

CHAPTER FIVE: Eugénie: The Marriage Market

95 Quoted in Ridley, p. 161.
96 Ridley, p. 156.
97 Sergeant, *Last Empress of the French*, p. 23
98 Chapman-Huston
99 CG, p. 343.
100 LF, p. 21-22.
101 Ridley, p. 156.
102 LF, p. 263.
103 Mérimée 16th Nov 1844 refers to 'your little boy Carlos'.
    LF CIII. Note 263 first babies often said to be premature if
    born before 9 months.
104 Tschudi, p. 29.
105 Aronson, Theo, *Royal Vendetta*, p. 33.
106 Challice, Rachel, *The Secret History of the Court of Spain*, p.
    148.
107 Bolitho, Hector, ed., *The Prince Consort and His Brother: Two
    Hundred New Letters*, p. 91.
108 Ibid., p. 83.
109 Ridley, p. 161.
110 Ibid.
111 Palmerston's diary, quoted in Sergeant, p. 34.
112 Evans, Thomas V., *Memoirs of Dr Thomas Evans*, p. 90.
113 Clarendon Deposit, MS Eng 2085, Folio 2.
114 Michener, James, Iberia, Vol. 2, p. 423.
115 *Memoires Dr Thos Evans*, p. 50.
116 Sergeant, p. 27.

117   Duff, p. 95; Stoddart, Jane T., *The Life of Empress Eugénie*, p. 38.
118   Alba, Barcelona lecture, Boletin de laReal Academia de Historia CXX 71 – 101 Madrid 1947.
119   Ibid.; Princess Pilar and Chapman-Huston, p. 10.
120   Woodham-Smith, Cecil, *Queen Victoria*, p. 442-443.
121   LF, p. 50.
122   AW Rait, *Prosper Mérimée*, p. 262.
123   Alba, Oxford lecture, pp. 21-22.
124   Fleury, vol. 1, p. 356.
125   Cowley to Russell 17th Jan 1853 RA Add 19/45. Quoted by the gracious permission of Her Majesty the Queen.
126   Ridley, p. 330.
127   Duff, p. 99.
128   Ridley, p. 344.
129   Stoddart, p. 29.

CHAPTER SIX: Margaret: Robert Starts Again

130   Wetzel County W.V. Obituaries, vol. 2,
131   Census of Manchester 30th March 1851. HO 157 2287
132   Census of Pennington 7 April 1861. RG9 2803.

CHAPTER SEVEN: Eugénie: The Imperial Marriage

133   Quoted in Sergeant, p. 165.
134   Stoddart, p. 41.
135   Sencourt, p. 86.
136   Duff, p. 81.
137   Tschudi, p. 163; Carette, p. 122.
138   LF, p. 203.
139   CG, vol. 7, p. 101, To Honore St Clair.
140   CG, vol. 7, p. 197.
141   Bolitho, Hector, and Baillie, A.V., eds., *Later Letters of Lady Augusta Stanley*, p. 115; CG, vol. 14, p. 493; Fleury, vol. 1, p. 15. This episode is not dated but the following page of these memoirs refers to Mérimée's appointment to the Senate.
142   CG, vol. 7, pp. 442, 445 and and Raitt p. 275.
143   CG, vol. 7.
144   Anonymous, *Uncensored Recollections*, p. 20.
145   Burchell, S.C., *Upstart Empire*, p. 310.
146   Tschudi, p. 193.

147   Carette, p. 293.
148   Ibid., pp. 179-180.
149   Weintraub, Stanley, *Victoria: An Intimate Biography*, p. 244.
150   Hibbert, Christopher, ed., *Queen Victoria in Her Letters and Journals*, p. 131.
151   Ibid., p. 133.
152   Ibid.
153   Longford, Elizabeth, *Victoria RI*, p. 354.
154   Clarendon Papers, Bodleian Library, Oxford. FO 361 Deposit 2057

CHAPTER NINE: Eugénie: The Dynasty is Assured

155   Carey, Agnes, *Empress Eugénie in Exile*, p. 21.
156   CG, vol. 8, p. 306.
157   Zeldin, Theodore, *The Political System of Napoleon III*, p. 104.
158   CG, vol. 8, p. 315.
159   CG, vol. 8, p. 325.
160   Kurtz, p. 103.
161   Longford, p. 189.
162   Fleury, p. 460.
163   Anonymous, *Uncensored Recollections*.
164   Vizetelly, p. 24.
165   Sergeant, p. 131.
166   Murat, p. 182.

CHAPTER ELEVEN: Eugénie: I Must Go To Manchester

167   PRO FO 519/228 6019.
168   Stoddart, p. 12.
169   Smyth, *Streaks of Life*.
170   Stoddart, p. 148.
171   CG, p. 69 (November 1860).
172   CG
173   CG, Mérimée to Jenny Dacquin. Footnote to p. 160 quotes Baroche, *Second Empire* p. 167
174   Baroche, Céleste, Madame Jules de, *Second Empire: Notes et Souvenirs*, p. 167, quoted in ibid.
175   Bronné, Carlo, *Lettres de Léopold Ier Roi des Belges*, p. 276.
176   Duff, p. 148.
177   Bolitho and Baillie, *Letters of Lady Augusta Bruce née Stanley*,

p. 152

178   Fulford, p. 282.

179   Duff, p. 147.

180   Fleury, vol. 1, p. 274.

181   Duff, p. 149.

182   Sencourt, p. 162, n. 1.

183   Stoddart, p. 146.

184   Malmesbury, James, Earl of, *Memoirs of an Ex-Minister*, p. 177.

185   Remembered but not found.

186   Sergeant, p. 264.

187   LF, p. 203.

188   *The Times*, 27 August 1995, p. 13.

189   O'Neile, John, *A Lancashire Weaver's Journal*.

190   Manchester *Examiner and Times*, 1 December 1860,

191   Fulford, Roger, ed., *Beloved Mama: Private Correspondence of Queen Victoria and the German Crown Princess*, p. 57.

192   Royal Leamington Spa Courier and Warwickshire Standard, 3 December 1860.

193   LF, p. 204.

194   Vizetelly, p. 174.

195   Fulford, *Dearest Child*, p. 288.

196   Kennedy, A.L. ed., *My Dear Duchess: Social and Political Letters to the Duchess of Manchester*, p. 120.

197   Ibid., p. 121.

198   Malmesbury, quoted in Sergeant, p. 265.

199   Kennedy, p. 133.

200   Bolitho and Baillie, p. 174.

201   Carette, p. 69.

202   CG, vol. 6, p. 324.

CHAPTER TWELVE: Margaret: Eugénie

203   Chapman-Huston, p. 258.

204   Carette.

205   LF, p. 204.

CHAPTER THIRTEEN: Eugénie: Elsewhere

206   CG, vol. 7, p. 182.

207   CG, vol. 7, p. 544.

208   Ibid.

209   *The Times*, Monday 22nd July 1867.
210   Clarendon letters vol 2, page 334.
211   Fulford, Roger, ed., *Your Dear Letter: Private Correspondence of Queen Victoria and the Crown Princess of Prussia, 1865-871*, p. 145.
212   On 12 August 1867 Lord Clarendon was in Wiesbaden, per Maxwell, vol. 2, p. 334.

CHAPTER FOURTEEN: Margaret: American Cousins

213   Personal communication from Forrest Hammersley.
214   RG9 1931 54, p. 1.
215   Christiansen, Rex, *A Regional History of the Railways of Great Britain*, vol. 7, p. 229.
216   Personal communication from Mrs Buckham of nearby Pendeford, who comes from a longstanding railway family.
217   Census of 1871; RG10 2923, p. 5.
218   Richardson, Neil, The Manchester Historical Recorder, p. 40.
219   Ibid.
220   Callahan, James M., *History of West Virginia Old and New*, vol. 3, p. 464.
221   New Martinsville Census, 1910, available in New Martinsville Public Library.
222   Wetzel County, W.V., Obituaries; information by courtesy of Elizabeth Mullet of the Wetzel County Genealogical Society.

CHAPTER FIFTEEN: Eugénie: The End of an Era

223   Sergeant, p. 36; Stoddart, p. 221.
224   Letter from Sir John Burgoyne, 13 September 1870, quoted by kind permission of Peter Spencer.
225   Raitt, p. 353.
226   CG, vol. 15, p. 167.
227   Stoeckl, Agnes, Baroness de, *When Men Had Time to Love*, p. 175.
228   Duff, p. 247.
229   Garets, p. 147.
230   Loliée, Frédéric, *Women of the Second Empire*, p. 283.
231   Princess Caroline My Memoires Murat, p. 314.
232   Tisdall, E.E.P., *The Prince Imperial*, p. 202.
233   Tschudi, p. 256.
234   Tisdall, p. 206.

235   Murat, p. 162.

236   Garets, p. 196.

237   Tisdall, p. 175

238   Garets, p. 223.

239   Tisdall, p. 175.

240   Duff, David, *The Shy Princess*, p. 153.

241   *The Century Magazine*, June 1893

242   Murat, p. 314.

243   Marie Louise, Princess, *My Memories of Six Reigns*, p. 189.

244   Tisdall, p. 201.

245   Bicknell, p. 195.

246   Tschudi, p. 256.

247   Fulford, *Beloved Mama*, p. 44.

248   Ibid., p. 47.

249   Tisdall, p. 193.

250   Garets, p. 271.

CHAPTER SIXTEEN: Margaret: Eugénie Again

251   Sergeant, p. 402.

252   Garets, p. 142.

253   Census of 1881, RG 11/2830 152, p. 28.

254   Garets, p. 140.

CHAPTER SEVENTEEN: Eugénie: Her Only Love

255   Aronson, Theo, *Princess Alice, Countess of Athlone*, p. 277.

256   CG, August 1869.

257   Fulford, *Your Dear Letter*, p. 209.

258   Petrie, p. 186.

259   Barker, p. 193.

260   Chapman-Huston, p. 10.

261   LF, Vol. 2, p. 217, footnote.

262   Challice, p. 271.

263   LF, Vol. 2, p. 28; see also note on p. 205.

264   Chapman-Huston, p. 9.

265   Garets, p. 223.

266   Cortés Cavanillas, Julian, *Alfonso XII*, p. 11.

267   LF, vol. 2., p. 135.

268   LF, vol. 2 p. 163

269   Duff, p. 280; Sencourt, p. 350.

CHAPTER EIGHTEEN: Letitia

270   CG, November 1850
271   CG, January 1851
272   Ridley, p. 322, cites *El Heraldo* 16 April 1851 and *La Epoca* 6
       April 1851.
273   Ridley, p. 322.
274   Wetzel County WV Obituaries, vol. 11, p. 82.

CHAPTER NINETEEN: Eugénie: Sisters

275   Sergeant, p. 402.
276   Longford, p. 344.
277   Carey, p. 173.
278   Ibid., p. 274.
279   Ridley, p. 619.
280   Weintraub.
281   LF, vol. 2, p. 163.
282   Tschudi.
283   Duff, David, *Queen Victoria's Highland Journals*, p. 12.
284   Bird, Dennis L., *Our Skating Heritage*, p. 284.
285   Carey, p. 152.
286   Smyth, p. 24.

CHAPTER TWENTY: Margaret: Margaret's Family

287   Occleshaw, Michael, *The Romanov Conspiracies*, p. 182.
288   Legge, p. 45-46.
289   Talbot, Edward, *LNWR Recalled*, p. 68.
290   Ibid., p. 116.
291   RG 11/2830, p. 28.
292   RG 11/2830 152, p. 29.
293   Talbot, *LNWR Recalled*, p. 68.
294   Talbot, Edward, Collected Writings Oxford Publications 1987
       The Locomotive Department, p. 65.
295   The 'Earles' may have been an Earl and Countess, such as the
       fourth Earl and Countess Manvers of Thoresby Hall. The third
       Countess, Georgine Jane Elizabeth Fanny de Franquetot, who
       was French, had died in July 1910. The daughter of Gustave,
       Duc de Coigny, she had received a Sevres vase as a wedding
       gift from Eugénie. Thoresby Hall, until its recent sale, con-
       tained souvenirs and several original paintings of Napoleon III
       and Eugénie, as well as the portrait of the Prince Imperial, still

on its easel.

296   Daudet, Lucien, *Dans l'Ombre de l'Impératrice Eugénie*, November 15th.

297   Ibid.

298   Information from the marriage register regarding J. Robert S. Cartlidge and Emily Gardner.

299   Ridley, p. 631.

300   1901 Census RG 132706

301   Cartlidge, Rev. J.E.G., *Newbold Astbury and Its History*, p. 17.

302   Armstrong, Nancy, *Fans*, p. 128.

CHAPTER TWENTY-ONE: Eugénie: The End and the Enigmas

303   Loliée, p. 285, note.

304   Personal conversation with Fr Magnus, Farnborough Abbey, 1998.

305   Vizetelly, p. 162.

306   Carette, p. 141.

307   Vizetelly, p. 162.

308   Kurtz, p. 368.

309   Ridley, p. xiii.

310   Woodham-Smith, p. 555.

311   Grosvenor, Loelia, Duchess of Westminster, *Grace and Favour*, p. 28.

312   Orbell, John, and Pressnell, L.S., *Guide to the Historical Records of British Banking*, p. xiii.

CHAPTER TWENTY-TWO: Conclusions

313   Legge, p. 307.

314   Lodey, Joey, *Family Tree* (vol. 2, No. 6), p. 7.

315   Walden, Brian, *The Sunday Times*, 23 August 1987

316   Briggs, Asa, 'The Open University', BBC Radio, 28 February 1998.

317   Personal communication from Jean Cartlidge.

318   Carette, pp. 179–180.

319   Garets, p. 151.

APPENDIX: The Letters

320   Raitt, p. 262.

321   LF, p. 17.

322   Parturier, p. 8.

323   Bolitho, *The Prince Consort.*

324   Fagan, Louis, ed., *Letters of Julius and Mary Mohl*, p. 80.

325   Clarendon Deposit, MSS C555, Bodleian Library, Oxford.

326   Garets, p. 140.

327   Barker, pp. 36–37.

328   Ponsonby, Sir Frederick, ed., *Letters of the Empress Frederick,*
        p. xvi.

Biographies

Ada, Princess Adelaide of Hohenlohe-Langenburg, a niece of Queen Victoria.

Alba, James 15th Duke of, Duke of Berwick, 12 times Grandee of Spain.

Alba, Carlos 16th Duke of, born 4th December.

Alba, James 17th Duke, Spanish Ambassador to Great Britain, 1939–1945.

Alcanises, Pepe, Marquis, later the Duke of Sexto, married the widow of the Duke of Morny, the illegitimate half-brother of Napoleon III. Restored Alfonso Xll to the Spanish throne.

Beatrice, Princess, youngest child of Queen Victoria.

Bonaparte, Louis Napoleon, the Emperor Napoleon III, son of Louis, King of Holland and Queen Hortense, nephew of the great Napoleon, born 1808, died 1873 at Camden Place, England.

Bonaparte, Prince Victor Napoleon, eldest son of Prince Napoleon (Plon Plon) named as his heir by the Prince Imperial. Died 1926.

Beyle, Henri, known as Stendhal the French writer.

Bocher Madame, *née* Aline Laborde, sister in law of Mme. Delessert.

Brown, John, Highland gillie personal servant and friend of Queen Victoria.

Bruce, Lady Augusta, later Stanley. Lady-in-waiting to the Duchess of Kent, mother of Queen Victoria.

Calderon, Estebanez (Serafin), Spanish writer, born 1799, died Madrid 1867.

Clarendon, Fourth Earl of, see Villiers, George William.

Cowley, Henry Wellesley, 1st Earl, British Ambassador to France. Born 1807, died 1884.

Delessert, Madame Gabriel, *née* Valentine Laborde, wife of the Prefect of French Police and mistress of Prosper Merimee. Born 1806, died 1894.

Evans, Doctor Thomas W., an American dentist working in Paris.

Eley, Marchioness of, Eugénie's oldest and closest friend in England, dating from her girlhood. Mistress of the Robes to, and a close friend of, Queen Victoria. Died 1890.

Ena, Princess, the daughter of Princess Beatrice and Prince Henry of Battenburg.

212

Filon, Augustin, secretary of the Empress Eugenie and tutor to the Prince Imperial. A biographer of Prosper Merimee.

Fleury, Emile Felix, Count and French General. Born 1815, died Paris, 1884.

Fleury Count Maurice, son of the above, published with Louis Sonolet 'La Societe du Second Empire'.

Flower, Miss, the English Governess of Paca and Eugenie de Montijo.

Fould, Achille, a Jewish protestant. Politician and banker, and a minister under Napoleon III.

Galve, Count, brother of the 15th Duke of Alba.

Hamilton, Duchess of, *née* Marie of Baden. Cousin of Napoleon III.

Hugenschmidt. Doctor, an illegitimate son of Napoleon III who was brought up by Dr. Evans, said to closely resemble the Emperor.

Isabella, Queen of Spain, born 1830, died 1904.

Kirkpatrick, Maria Manuela, Countess of Montijo, daughter of Baron de Grivengee, mother of Paca and Eugenie. Mistress of George Villiers who later became Lord Clarendon.

Laborde Madame Leon, wife of Madame Valentine Delessert's brother.

Lucas (Don) de Gracia y Gutierrez, Majo Domo of Madame de Montijo.

Mérimée Prosper, French writer and traveller, lifelong mentor and friend of Madame de Montijo and her daughters, born 1803, died 1870 at Cannes.

Mohl Madame, born Mary Clarke, in Westminster, 1793. Married Julius Mohl, 7 years her junior, after the age of 50. Began her celebrated 'Friday evenings' in her house Rue du Bac, after 1847. A friend of Mérimée and of Madame Gabriel Delessert, had a total enmity of Louis Napoleon.

Montijo, Count of, Don Cipriano Guzman y Palalfox y Porto Carrero, Count of Teba, second son of the Count of Monitjo, Grandee of Spain, married Maria Manuela Kirkpatrick, 15th Dec. 1817, died 15th March 1839. Became Count of Montijo on the death of his brother.

Montijo, Marie Eugénia Ignace Augustin Guzman y Palafox Countess of Teba (Eugenie), born 5th May 1826 married the Emperor Napoleon III January 1853, died July 1920.

Montijo Maria Francisca de Sales (Paca), elder sister of Eugenie and wife of the 15th Duke of Alba, died September 1861.

Morny Duke of, the illegitimate half brother of Napoleon III. The son of their mother, Hortense.

Morny Duchess of, *née* Sophie Troubetzkoi, when widowed became the wife of Pepe Alcanises, Duke of Sexto.

Napoleon Louis, the Prince Imperial, son of Napoleon III and Eugénie. Born 1856, died 1879.

Panizzi, Sir Anthony, an Italian born 1797 died 1879, became Chief Librarian of the British Museum, a friend of Merimee and of the Emperor and Empress of France.

Primoli, Count Joseph, son of Prince Charles Bonaparte, a friend of Eugénie in her latter years. Died in 1927.

Pilar, Infanta, sister of Alfonso XII. 2nd daughter of Queen Isabel.
Rogers, the Misses. four sisters who ran a school for young ladies in Clifton Bristol.

Russell, Lord John, British Prime Minister, 1846-52 and 1865-66. Born 1792, died 1878.

Sencourt Robert, the *nom de plume* of Professor Robert Esmond Gordon George, wrote a biography of Eugenie in conjunction with the 17th Duke of Alba.

Sharpe, Sutton, English lawyer and playboy, a friend of Mérimée and Henry Beyle (Stendhal) lived at 10 Nottingham Place, Marylebone, son of a brewer, born 1797, died 22nd February 1843.

Villiers, George William, later 4th Earl of Clarendon, British Ambassador in Paris and in Madrid, born 1800 married the daughter of the first Earl of Verulam, a widow, died 22nd June, 1870. Lover of Madame de Montijo and possibly the father of Eugénie.

Xifre Madame Julia, born 1801, died 1868, wife of a wealthy merchant of Barcelona and a friend of Madame de Montijo.

Bibliography

Alba, Duke of. *La Emperatriz Eugenia.*
Alba, Duke of. *Lectures 'The Ark', Oxford l94l.* Barcelona, 1947.
Aronson, Theo. *Napoleon III Family Background.*
Aronson, Theo. *The Fall of the Third Napoleon.*
Ashton, Joseph. *Picture of Manchester.* Didsbury re-print, 1969.
Aspin, Chris. *The Cotton Industry.* Shire Publications Ltd., 1981.
Astbury Women's Institute. *Astbury Now and Then.* Astbury, 1980.
Barker, Nancy N. *Distaff Diplomacy.* Austin Texas, 1967.
Bee, Malcolm. *Industrial and Social Reform in the Manchester Region.*
Bibesco, Princess. *The Prince Imperial. 'A Fantasia'.*
Bicknell, Anna. *Life in the Tuileries under the Second Empire.*
Bolitho, Hector. *The Prince Consort (200 Letters to His Brother).* London, 1933.
Buchanan Meriel. *Victorian Gallery.*
Burchell, S. C. *Upstart Empire.*
Bury, J. P. T. *Napoleon III and the Second Empire.*
Carette (née Bouvet) *My Mistress the Empress Eugénie.*
Carey, Agnes. *Empress Eugénie in Exile.*
Carley, T. A. B. *Democratic Despot. Life of Napoleon III.* London, 1961.
Cartlidge, Rev. John E. Gordon. *Newbold Astbury and its History.* Thomas Gordon, 1915.
Castellane, Marquis de. *Confessions of the Marquis de Castellane.* Thornton Butterworth, 1924.
Challice, Rachael. *Secret History of Court of Spain.* John Long, 1909.
Cole Hubert. *The Betrayers.* Eyre Methuen, 1972.
Christiansen, Rex. *Regional History of the Railways of Great Britain volume 7.*
Coleridge, Henry James.
Cooper Duff. *Talleyrand.*
Cortes, Cavanillas *Alfonso XII* Atenas AG Escoral 135 Barcelona, 1961.
Corti Egon Caesar. *The English Empress.*
Craven, Mrs Augustus. *Lady Georgiana Fullerton*
Daudet, Lucien. *Dans l'ombre de l'Imperatrice Eugénie.*

Daudet, Mme Alphonse. *Lettres in Times.*
Duff, David. *Eugénie and Napoleon III.* Collins. 1978.
Duff, David. *The Shy Princess.*
Dunlop, Ian. *Royal Palaces of France.*
Elliot, Frances. *Diary of an Idle Woman in Spain.*
Eugénie, Empress. *Lettres Familières de l'Imperatrice Eugénie.* (ed Alba). Paris 1935.
Evans, T. W. *Memoirs of Dr. Thos. Evans.* London. 1905.
Fagan, Louis Alexander. *The Life of Sir Anthony Panizzi KCB.*
Field, J. (Anon.) *Uncensored Recollections.*
Filon. *Recollections of the Empress Eugénie.* London, 1920.
Filon. *The Prince Imperial.* 1913.
Fleury, Comte. *Memoirs of the Empress Eugénie.* D. Appleton and Co., 1920.
Ford, Richard. *Gatherings from Spain.*
Garets, Comtesse des. *The Tragic Empress.* Skeffington & Son.
Gillies, A. D. *Those Dark Satanic Mills.* Wigan R.O., 1981
Gooch, G. P. *The Second Empire.*
Guest, Ivor. *Napoleon III in England.* London, 1952.
Gunnell, Doris. *Sutton Sharpe et Ses Amis Francais.*
Head, Robert. *History of Congleton.*
Holt, Edgar. *Plon Plon: The Life of Prince Napoleon.* 1973.
Hurst and Blackett. *Conversations with Distinguished People During the Second Empire.*
Hyde, Francis, *Liverpool.*
Illustrated London News, The.
John, Katherine. *The Prince Imperial.* London, 1939.
Kaye, M. M. *The Golden Calm.*
Kennedy, A.L. (editor). *My Dear Duchess.* John Murray London. 1956.
Koengh. *La Livre de la Famille Imperial.*
Krieger, Eric. *Bygone Manchester.*
Kurtz, Harold. *The Empress Eugénie.* H. Hamilton London, 1964.
Legge, E. *The Empress Eugénie and her son.* London 1916
Leigh Local History Society. *An Outline History of Leigh.*
Leopold, Roi des Belges, *Lettres.* (Ed. Carlo Bronne.)
Lines, Charles. 'Napoleon III's days in the Midlands', *Birmingham Post.* 2nd January 1973.
Little, Brian. *Clifton's Eugénie House.* Bristol 1978.
Loliee, Frederic. *Gilded Beauties of the Second Empire.* 1919
Loliee, Frederic. *Women of the Second Empire and the Court of Napoleon III.* John Land and the Bodley Head, 1907.

Lunn, John. *Atherton*.

Lytton, Lady. *Court Diary*. Edited Mary Lutyens.

Malmsbury, Lord. *Memoirs of an ex Minister*.

Manchester Central Library. *Local Studies*.

Manchester Examiner and Times. Nov–Dec 1860.

Manchester Guardian. Dec 1860.

Manchester Local History Library. *Men and Women of Manchester*.

Marie Louise, Princess. *My Memories of Six Reigns*.

Martineau, M. *Lettres à Stendhal*. Tome 3.

Maxwell. *The life and letters of George William Frederick, Fourth Earl of Clarendon*.

McKinley, Richard. *The Surnames of Lancashire*. Leopard's Head Press. 1981.

Mérimée, Prosper. *Correspondence Generale* (17 volumes). Privat Toulouse.

Mérimée, Prosper. *Lettres a la famille Delessert*. Paris, Plon. 1931.

Mérimée, Prosper. *Lettres a Mme. de Montijo*.

Mérimée, Prosper. *Lettres de Parturier*.

Mérimée, Prosper. *Lettres inconnue*. Michel Levy freres, 1897.

Mérimée, Prosper. *Mosaique*. Paris, 1888.

Mohl, Julius and Mary. *Letters* edited by Louis Fagan, London, 1877.

Morly, Diana de. *Worth*.

Mostyn, Dorothy. *Farnborough Hill, the Story of a House*.

Murat, Princess Caroline. *My Memoirs*. viii

North, Peat Anthony B. *Gossip from Paris during the Second Empire*.

O'Neile, John. *A Lancashire Weaver's Journal*. Nottingham Library. 942 7685.

Paleologue, Maurice. *Les Entretiens de L'Imperatrice Eugénie*.

Pemberton, Robert. *History Of Pleasants County*. Oracle Press W. Virginia,1929.

Petrie, Charles. *The Spanish Royal House*.

Pilar, Princess and Chapman, Huston. *Alfonso XIII*.

Ponsonby, Arthur. *Henry Ponsonby, Queen Victoria's Private Secretary: His Life from His Letters*. Macmillan, 1943.

Pressnell, L.S. and Orbell, John. *British Banking*.

Primolo, Comte. *L'enfance d'une Souveraine*. *Revue des Deux Mondes*. Paris. 1923.

Raitt, A.W. *Prosper Mérimée*. 1932.

Redford, Arthur. *Manchester Merchants and Foreign Trade*.

Reed, Brian. *Crewe to Carlisle*.

Richardson, Joanna. *La Vie Parisienne: Portrait of a Bonaparte*.

Richardson, Neil. *The Manchester Historical Recorder*.

Ridley, Jasper. *Napoleon III and Eugénie*. Constable, 1979.

Robertson, Alan W. *Post Roads, Towns and Rates*. Re-print. 1961.

Royal Leamington Spa Courier and Warwicks Standard.

Sencourt, R. *The Life of the Empress Eugénie*. London, 1931.

Sergeant, Philip W. *Last Empress of the French*.

Sharpe, Samuel. *Lettres de Mérimée et Sutton Sharpe*.

Shercliff, W.H. *Manchester*.

Simpson, F. A. *Life of the Prince Imperial*.

Simpson, M. C. M. *Letters and Recollections of Julius and Mary Mohl*.

Smyth, Ethyl. *Streaks of Life*. London, 1921.

Stanley, Lady Augusta *née* Bruce. *Letters of, and further letters of.* (ed. Albert Baillie.)

Stendhal. *Courier Anglais*.

Stendhal. *Lettres a Tome III 1835-42*. Ed. M. Martineau.

Stendhal. *Private Diaries*. Ed. Robert Page.

Stoddart, Jane T. *The Life of the Empress Eugénie*.

Stoekl, Agnes de. *When Men Had Time to Love*.

Strachey, Lytton. *Queen Victoria*. Chatto and Windus, 1922

Talbot, E. L. *N.W.R Miscellany* (2 volumes.)

J. M. Thomas, *Louis Napoleon and the Second Empire*. Oxford, 1954.

Thompson, J. M. *Louis Napoleon and the Second Empire*. Basil Blackwell, 1954.

Thompson, W. H. *History of Manchester*. Thompson, 1967.

Times, The.

Tisdall, E. E. P. *The Prince Imperial*.

Torriglia, Llanos y. *Maria Manuela de Montijo*. Madrid, 1932.

Trelawny. *The Emperor and Miss Howard*.

Tschudi ,Clara. *Eugénie, Empress of the French*.

Turnbull, Patrick, *Eugénie of the French*.

Victoria, Queen, *Her Letters and Journals*. A selection by Christopher Hibbert.

Victoria, Queen. *Journal*. Edited by David Duff.

Victoria, Queen. *Journals*. Royal Archives.

Victoria, Queen. *My Dearest Child*. Evans, London, 1964.

Victoria, Queen. *Private Correspondence to the German Crown Princess*. Edited by Roger Fulford (5 vols.).

Villa Urrutia, Marques de. *Eugenia de Guzman*. Espasa Calpe, 1932.

Villiers, G. A. *Vanished Victorian: Life of George. the fourth Earl of Clarendon*.

Vizetelly, E. A. (Le petit homme rouge.) *The Court of the Tuileries*. London, 1907.

Weintraub, Stanley. *Queen Victoria, Biography of*. 1986.

Westminster. Leola, Duchess of. *Grace and Favour.*
Williams, Ned. *Railways* (2 volumes).
Williams, Roger L. *Gaslight and Shadow.*
Woodham Smith, Cecil. *Queen Victoria.*
Zeldin, T. *The Political System of Napoleon III.*

Acknowledgements

My long-suffering family who for so many years have lived with Eugénie de Montijo.

The late Mrs Ann Hammersley for her early editing.

The late Jasper Ridley for information.

Julian Robinson of the History Department of Nottingham University, for the loan of books.

Andrew Nickolds, for professional advice

The Staff of The Arts Library, Nottingham Central Library,

A.D. Gillies, Archivist, Leigh, Lancs.

The late Frank Cartlidge for information concerning the Astbury Cartlidges.

Mrs Francoise Pate for checking my translations of Mérimée 1840–43.

The late Mrs Inelia Avila for reading and translating Llanos de Torriglia's 'Maria Manuela Kirkpatrick'.

Angela Houston for searching the railway archives.

The Right Hon the 7th Earl of Clarendon for permission to quote from the letters of the 4th Earl.

The Reverend Dean of Astbury.

The Reverend Hinton of Bushbury.

The Superintendent Registrars of Leigh, Manchester, Warrington, Walsall, and Wolverhampton.

The Bristol Local Studies Library.

The late W.G. Fieldgate.

Brian Little.

Congleton Local Studies Library.

Walsall Central Library and Local Studies Dept.

Mrs Buckham of Pendeford, Staffs. for information regarding the local railway.

The National Railway Museum. York.

Yvonne Ash of the Nottingham Records Office.

Jean Barnes of the Warrington Family History Society.

London and North Western Railway Society.

Miguel de Avendano.

The Right Hon the Earl of Clarendon for permission to quote from the Clarendon papers in the Bodelian Library.

Victoria Sanders of Philips Auctioneers.

The Archivist, Windsor Castle.
The Public Records Office.
The Principal Registry, St. Catherine's House.
The Census Office Portugual Street
Mrs Marie MacFarlane.
The late Mrs Jean Cartlidge.
Mrs Barbara Perry (*née* Cartlidge.)
The Staff of the Local History Library, Manchester.
The Local History Librarian, Congleton.
The Local History Librarian, Wolverhampton.
The Local History Librarian, Leigh.
Dr. J. Laidlar, Newspaper Librarian, John Rylands Library, University of Manchester.
The Regional Information Librarian, Leamington Spa.
The Picture Library, Illustrated London News.
Foreign Office Records Dept.
The Public Records Office, .
The Cultural Attache, The Spanish Embassy.
The Archivist Messrs Baring Bros.
The Cheshire Records Office.
The Editor, The Voice of the West, Bristol.
Mrs Julie Bowen.
John Hewitt, Trumpet St., Manchester.
Eileen Hudsdable.
The Vicars of Pennington, Leigh, and Coven.
The Archivist, Hampshire Record Office.
Her Majesty the Queen for her gracious permission to quote from a letter from Lord Cowley to Lord John Russell.
Peter Spencer.
Mrs Hughes Sec Lancs Fam Hist. Soc.
Diane Bevan.
Albert Douglas Pemberton Cartlidge.
Heather Carole nee Pemberton Cartlidge.

Elizabeth Estlack Mullet of Wetzel Co. Genealogical Society, USA
Ohio Public Library, USA
New Martinsville Library, USA
Belmont County Chapter, USA
Ohio Genealogical Society, USA
Martins Ferry Public Library, USA

The very many other friends and acquaintances who have shown interest and been so helpful with various aspects of my researches.

Joyce Cartlidge was born in 1926 in Derby, but moved shortly after to Nottingham where she has lived most of her life. She won a scholarship to Mundella Grammar School but due to wartime conditions was only able to complete 2 ½ years there.

Prior to marriage in 1947 she worked for her father, a motor engineer and garage owner. For most of her married life she has assisted her husband in his practice as consultant chartered builder and surveyor.

Joyce is a long-standing member of The Inner Wheel Club (linked to the Rotary Club). having served as President for both the Wollaton Park and Newark Branches. Her hobbies include horse riding, ice skating, family history and caravanning.

She has two children, a son and a daughter, both of whom are married.

Printed in the United Kingdom
by Lightning Source UK Ltd.
134358UK00001B/6/P